THE ART OF SELECTING A JURY

by

THE HONORABLE ROBERT A. WENKE
Judge of the Superior Court
for the County of Los Angeles

AVAILABLE FROM
PARKER & SON
P.O. BOX 22017
LOS ANGELES, CALIFORNIA 90022
$12.00 PER COPY
CALIFORNIA RESIDENT 6% SALES TAX

Parker & Son, Inc.
1979

ACKNOWLEDGMENT

There is a proverb to the effect that "you judge a trapper by his pelts." With this thought in mind I solicited the assistance of the lawyers and judges listed below, all of whom have proved by their performance that they are masters of the art of jury selection. They graciously consented to critique my work. Their incisive comments and suggestions, reflecting the wisdom gained through years of practical experience, were invaluable. This handbook reflects their thinking. I deeply appreciate their help. Our profession is indebted to them for their willingness to share with others the knowledge and insight they acquired through hard work and determination.

Hon. Harold J. Ackerman
Hon. F. Ray Bennett
Franics R. Bergmann
Peter R. Bregman
Joseph H. Cummins
Douglas Dalton
Everett E. Demler
Warren L. Ettinger
Hon. D. Sterry Fagan
David Feldman
Paul J. Fitzgerald
Edward P. George, Jr.
David R. Glickman
Browne Greene
Jack E. Grisham
G. Dana Hobart
Clarence S. Hunt
Hon. James M. Ideman
H. Gilbert Jones
Hon. John A. Loomis
Elmer Low
Leon Mayer
Hon. Eugene McClosky
Michael J. Montagna
Anthony Murray
Albert C. S. Ramsey
Mark P. Robinson
Roy V. Saukkola
Karl Seuthe
Theodore P. Shield
George E. Wise

I am also indebted to those who have written on this subject in years past. This vast fund of source material was indeed helpful in providing a core from which this book evolved.

Robert A. Wenke

ABOUT THE AUTHOR

Robert A. Wenke was graduated from the University of Nebraska School of Law. He engaged in the general practice of law in Long Beach, California, for approximately thirteen years, during which time he tried many jury cases, both criminal and civil. Since 1966 he has served as a Judge of the Superior Court for the County of Los Angeles, including two years as Presiding Judge, 1975-1976.

Judge Wenke has written a number of articles in the field of judicial administration, as well as an evidence handbook and a form book for property settlement agreements. He served as a member of the American team in the Anglo-American Legal Exchange of 1973. Presently he serves as a director of the American Judicature Society and the National Center for State Courts.

FOREWORD

I have endeavored to set forth in a concise, accessible, and easily understood manner generally accepted rules and principles to be used in selecting a jury.

The process of selecting a jury is commonly referred to as "voir dire", a French phrase meaning "true talk." Knowledge of the process stems chiefly from the perception of trial lawyers. In compiling this manual, I was fortunate in having the assistance of thirty-one experienced trial lawyers and judges who carefully reviewed my work and made numerous valuable suggestions. In the interest of brevity I have used the masculine gender as a generic term which includes both men and women.

Selecting a jury is educated guesswork. Every generalization concerning human behavior is laden with exceptions. People reflect a composite of factors: sex, age, race, occupation, personal experience, all of which in varying degrees have an impact on attitudes. Even if it were possible to assess the effect of all the things that influence the thinking of jurors no trial judge would allow counsel the time necessary to uncover them all. Further, given the knowledge we have, considered in the context of the arena in which a lawyer functions, there is no guarantee that mastery of the art will lead to victory in a given case. But, in the long run mastery of that art will increase the chances for success.

A virtual unanimity of opinion exists about many of the matters included; concerning other matters, there is only a consensus. Where there was only consensus, suggestions are something less than imperative. I omitted some matters because I was unable with any sense of confidence to take a definitive position.

Some contemporary writers on this subject advocate an intensely personal approach; one that attempts to delve deeply into the psyche of prospective jurors. The lawyers who critiqued the manuscript for this book do not concur. However, there undoubtedly is a place for such an approach where public feeling is both intense and unfavorable. Such trials probably constitute substantially less than one percent of all jury trials. This book is not written for that kind of trial wherein the jury selection process occupies many days or weeks.

I did not undertake to discuss specific rules and practices governing the selection of a jury in each jurisdiction. The variations among different jurisdictions, the process of change, and the turnover within the judiciary makes it impractical to do so. However, I have provided guidance to facilitate the acquisition of this indispensable knowledge. I also did not include sets of questions for every conceivable kind of trial; for example, eminent domain and commercial cases. Nevertheless, the material I have included should provide the base for formulating an adequate set of questions for almost any case. Of course, there always is litigation presenting unique features, requiring the exercise of ingenuity on the part of counsel. In any event, I believe this handbook can be a useful aid in selecting juries in all types of cases, regardless of their nature or complexity.

In conclusion, I recognize there will be differences of opinion about some of the statements contained herein. Certainly this is a subject about which reasonable people may differ. In any event, I believe utilization of this book will point the way to its improvement. Constructive criticism is most welcome. My address is 415 West Ocean Boulevard, Long Beach, California 90802.

Please let me hear from you.

ROBERT A. WENKE

ONTENTS

CONTENTS

Page

Page

Page

Page

Page

QUESTIONS FOR SPECIAL SITUATIONS

THE THREE APPROACHES TO VOIR DIRE

There are three approaches to voir dire: by the court exclusively, by the court and counsel, by counsel exclusively. It is important to familiarize yourself with the procedures followed in your state and the particular preferences of judges before whom you appear. Other lawyers, court staff, or a preliminary conference with the judge can provide you with this knowledge.

BY THE COURT EXCLUSIVELY

The judge makes introductory remarks and asks all the questions. Counsel may suggest questions to be asked; these should be written in advance, using simple sentences and commonly understood words.

As a part of its introduction, the court often expresses appreciation to the jurors for their service, explains the purpose of voir dire, briefly describes the nature of the case, introduces counsel and parties, announces the estimated length of the trial, spells out the manner in which the voir dire will be conducted, and indicates the various areas of inquiry.

Following this, the court questions prospective jurors individually and collectively as it deems appropriate. Generally, the court includes some explanation of applicable general principles of law and extracts commitments from jurors to follow the law and serve fairly and impartially.

BY THE COURT AND COUNSEL

The judge makes introductory remarks and asks some questions. Generally, the court elicits standard background information concerning each juror: occupation; occupation of spouse and adult children; residence; prior jury experience; claims for injuries; acquaintance with counsel, parties, witnesses; etc. Counsel are then given an opportunity to ask additional questions.

It is my opinion that this is the best approach. Specifically, the court should inquire into all relevant background facts and into the matter of disqualification on grounds of implied bias, such as relationship to a party. Counsel should inquire into actual bias, that is, into attitudes, opinions, and prejudices.

BY COUNSEL EXCLUSIVELY

The court may make introductory remarks or allow counsel to do so. Counsel then conduct the entire questioning process.

RULES AND POLICIES

Rules and policies applicable to jury selection vary from jurisdiction to jurisdiction. As a trial lawyer familiarize yourself with the basic procedures followed in the courtroom from the swearing of prospective jurors upon their arrival in the courtroom to answer questions about their qualifications, to the swearing in of those ultimately selected to serve.

In particular, make it a point to know:

a. The order in which attorneys for the parties question prospective jurors and exercise peremptory challenges.

b. Whether questioning is of the entire panel in the box or of one juror at a time.

c. Acceptable grounds for challenge for cause.

d. The number of peremptory challenges allowed each party. (In some jurisdictions peremptory challenges in civil cases are allotted according to sides. There may be more than one party on a side. If so, challenges may be divided among the parties, exercised jointly, or exercised on both a joint and an individual basis.)

e. Whether a challenge is lost if the right to challenge is not exercised in turn.

f. Whether you can challenge a juror whom you have previously accepted after the opposing side has exercised a challenge subsequent to your acceptance.

g. What questions are objectionable in voir dire.

h. How to object to improper voir dire.

Some jurisdictions limit the scope of voir dire to areas related to challenge for cause and will not permit examination conducted solely for the purpose of exercising peremptory challenges. However, prejudice is always a basis for a challenge for cause, and ordinarily you can make your inquiry into prejudice broad enough to elicit information that will be helpful in exercising peremptory challenges.

Judges within the same jurisdiction differ widely about what they allow and how they interpret restrictions on voir dire. It is your responsibility to become familiar with the policies and idiosyncrasies of the trial judge, with local court rules, and with applicable law. If the court conducts all voir dire, find out how and when you may submit questions for the court's consideration.

The trial judge has a duty to restrict unduly repetitious and unnecessary examination and to keep the examination within reasonable bounds. Always request a preliminary conference with the court if you have any uncertainty respecting permissible/objectionable voir dire. If at all possible, avoid confrontations with the court in the presence of jurors.

Generally speaking, trial judges disapprove of questions that attempt to instruct jurors about the law, except as to burden of proof and presumption of innocence.

Many judges do not like open-ended questions, that is, questions that generate discussion, because they are more time consuming and produce more challenges than leading questions. Open discussion can also be embarrassing to a self-conscious juror.

Excluding a proper question is more likely to constitute prejudicial error than allowing an improper question to be asked.

In every case consider the advisability of selecting alternate jurors or, in lieu thereof, entering into a stipulation for a verdict by a lesser number of jurors.

OUTLINE OF SELECTION PROCEDURE

1. The court announces the name of the case and asks if all sides are ready.

2. The court directs the clerk to swear the panel.

3. The clerk swears the panel and upon direction of the court draws twelve names at random. These jurors take their seats in the jury box immediately after each name is called.

4. The court makes its introductory statement, then asks such questions as it deems appropriate.

5. Counsel interrogate the prospective jurors. (Generally, the plaintiff in a civil case and the defendant in a criminal case question all twelve jurors first.)

6. Counsel generally challenge for cause as the cause arises during the questioning process. Ordinarily the reason for challenge is obvious, the juror is excused forthwith, and a replacement is called immediately. If a doubt arises over the propriety of a challenge for cause, the court defers its ruling until opposing counsel has had an opportunity to interrogate the juror. Hearings on challenges for cause should be conducted at the side bench outside the hearing of the jury.

7. Peremptory challenges are exercised as follows:
   a. They are exercised alternately, the plaintiff in a civil case and the prosecution in a criminal case proceeding first.

b. The number of challenges remaining to a side is not reduced by a failure to exercise a challenge in turn. However, when all sides pass on the same turn, the selection process is deemed completed.

c. Where there are several parties on a side, the court must resolve the following matters:

   1. the order in which parties will proceed on a given side,
   2. the effect of a party's failure to exercise its right to challenge,
   3. the right of a party to exercise unused challenges of another party on the same side, and
   4. the division of the total number of challenges allotted a side among the parties on that side. (This may involve the use of joint as well as individual challenges.)

8. The jury is sworn.

9. Alternate jurors are then selected in the same fashion, with additional challenges usually allowed by the court.

10. Alternate jurors are sworn.

INTRODUCTORY REMARKS

After the court indicates that counsel is to proceed, you the attorney rise (some very successful lawyers prefer to sit, believing it enhances informality and ease of conversation), address the court ("May it please the court"), walk over in front of the jury and address them. Suggested salutations: "Ladies and gentlemen of the jury panel"; "Members of the jury panel"; "Good morning, members of the jury panel (ladies and gentlemen); my name is ____________________, and I represent the plaintiff/defendant (name of client)."

Though introductory remarks are not an opening statement, they should include, to the extent not covered by the court, an introduction of yourself and your client; the names of your witnesses; the general nature of the litigation, including a brief description of the occurrence out of which the lawsuit arose; the estimated length of the case; and preparation for the questions to come. Indicate, for example, that questions will be asked about marital status, employment, accidents and injuries, involvement in litigation, etc. Make it clear that your objective is not to pry into personal affairs but only to gain information that will give the court and counsel an idea whether they, the prospective jurors, can be impartial in this particular case. Indicate further that you must ask questions about associations and experiences to learn if there are any which might cause a prospective juror to subconsciously favor one side. (At this point some lawyers tell jurors that they exercise challenges in order to achieve a balanced jury in terms of sex, age, occupation, etc.) Stress the importance of honest answers. State that everyone, including judges and lawyers, has some bias (you might refer to one or more of your own), and that no juror has reason to be upset or embarrassed if challenged.

At the conclusion of your introductory remarks, if the court has not already done so, touch upon the relationship between you and your client and the jurors. Make sure jurors understand communication is not permitted outside the courtroom and they should not feel slighted if neither the lawyers nor the clients speak with them. Otherwise, jurors might regard failure to exchange greetings with them as a personal insult. (Try to persuade the court amenities such as "hello" or "good morning" should be permitted; otherwise, if you make an inadvertent slip during a recess or adjournment a juror may judge you to be unethical.)

CONDUCT OF CLIENT AND COUNSEL

CLIENT

A client should be neat and clean, not flashy or overdressed. He should keep his hands in his lap or at his sides, be attentive but relaxed, be interested in the answers of all jurors, and be pleasant and confident in appearance.

A client should not chew gum, wear dark glasses, read, or react to answers of jurors orally or with facial expressions or gestures.

A client should be seated so jurors can look at him without staring directly at him. Ordinarily, however, a client with horrible injuries, for example, amputations, bad visible scars, or paraplegia, should not be present during voir dire.

A client should not nod or shake his head in response to a question put to him by you about a juror. Ask him to write — a simple "good" or "bad" will suffice — or to indicate on your jury sheet any he objects to. Many lawyers do not ask clients about individual jurors but, instead, ask them if there is anyone they want to excuse. You may want to provide a notebook for your client to assist him in recording his reactions.

COUNSEL

Be courteous, reasonable, sincere; be yourself. While you may ingratiate yourself by acts of kindness as appropriate occasions arise, do not make public requests to improve the comfort of individual jurors. Make acts of kindness subtle. Exaggerated courtesy and obvious flattery of women jurors are usually counterproductive. Treat all jurors with equal consideration; avoid discriminating between male and female jurors. Attempts at currying favor of particular jurors generally fall flat because they are so obvious.

Do not be condescending in manner or language; be polite without being obsequious. Jurors resent language which is above their comprehension or below their level of intelligence. Avoid, when possible, the use of legal words, such as "preponderance." For example, use "fault" rather than "liability" or "negligence." If it is necessary to use legal terminology, explain it in terms that lay persons ordinarily use.

Humor, if natural, is good. It does not necessarily involve the telling of stories. Avoid caustic wit, as well as forced humor. Be able to laugh at yourself.

Listen carefully to the correct pronunciation of a juror's name. Write it phonetically if necessary. Never make jokes about difficulty encountered in pronouncing or spelling a name. Many people are sensitive about their names.

Avoid embarrassing jurors. If you personally know a juror, even slightly, openly acknowledge it rather than chance the possibility of the juror's remaining quiet and the fact coming out later. Failure to reveal that you do know him can prove to be embarrassing. If a juror has a menial job do not make undue reference to that fact. If you should embarrass a juror, excuse him.

When it is natural to do so, personalize references to your client; for example say "Joe Brown" rather than "Mr. Brown," or "my client," or "the defendant." If, however, you are much younger than your client, familiar or informal address may be awkward. In any event, don't refer to your client in a way that makes you feel uncomfortable. Never refer to a client by his first name only unless the client is a minor or young adult.

Keep legible notes. If necessary, but not too often, politely interrupt proceedings or statements to secure correct information.

QUESTIONING STYLE

DEMEANOR AND APPROACH

Be informal, polite, friendly, dignified, interested, and natural. Natural, spontaneous humor, not overdone or forced, is good. Speak conversationally and maintain eye contact.

Be courteous at all times towards the court, the jury, and opposing counsel.

Use good but simple English; avoid slang. Ask straightforward questions. If it is necessary to use an unusual word or phrase, explain it. Avoid lengthy or overly technical questions. Use "please" and "thank you."

Be direct, yet diplomatic. Ask, for example, "Is it Miss, Ms., or Mrs. J?" instead of "Are you married?"; "Mrs. J, is there presently a Mr. J?" (This covers divorcees as well as widows.) Never ask a pregnant woman if she is a Miss or Mrs.

If you are unsure of how a juror pronounces his name, ask.

Proceed expeditiously; minimize tedium; avoid repetition. Listen carefully to the questions the court and opposing counsel ask and to the answers given. It is bad form to interrupt and ask, for example, "What did you say your occupation was?"

If you have the first opportunity to question jurors, address some individual questions to each juror, even if briefly.

As far as practical outline your questions in advance. However, some questions, such as follow-up questions, must be responsive to preceding answers.

Vary your questioning approach. Use group as well as individual questions. Vary the form and order of questions. Inject new questions from time to time.

Voir dire should consist of a mix of individual and group questions. Avoid questioning individual jurors in total sequence; memorize their names and skip around, provided the court permits it.

Individual questions are more conducive to candid responses than group questions.

If other counsel have preceded you it may not be necessary to question every juror individually. General questions addressed to the entire panel, or a combination of general and individual questions addressed to a portion of the panel, may suffice.

Group questioning saves time and reduces boredom and irritation. Use group questioning to educate jurors and to obtain certain kinds of information, such as "Have any of you ever been a witness in a criminal case?"

WINNING WAYS

If you can do so unobtrusively, memorize jurors' names. It not only enhances your rapport with the jury but also tends to build the jury's confidence in your memory. This confidence is helpful in final argument when you are discussing evidence, particularly if there is a disagreement between you and opposing counsel about what has transpired during the trial.

Address jurors by name. If you do it too frequently, however, it may irritate them. Limit such use to two or three times per juror.

Acknowledge that you are repeating some questions they've heard in other cases, but point out that you and your client have not had the benefit of hearing the answers.

To minimize the chances of making a juror appear foolish, use questions that suggest the answer.

Admit to your own prejudices, the jurors won't feel inferior if they admit to some.

Avoid the trite "Can you be fair?"

Such phrases as "naturally, you understand," "of course you know," and "as you realize," even if not literally true, generate good rapport.

Smile occasionally. Get a smile from the jurors.

When you can do so adroitly, dignify the work a juror performs; for example, say "maintenance worker" rather than "janitor". Ordinarily you may refer to a juror's occupation in the same way he does without incurring any offense.

If a juror takes obvious pride in his work, give him an opportunity to talk about it.

At the appropriate times, state unequivocally your and your client's complete satisfaction with the jurors in the box: "Plaintiff/defendant will accept the jury as now constituted, Your Honor." Even if, in fact, the client does not participate in the challenging process, you will find it desirable to go through the formality of conferring with him so that jurors know the client approves of their selection.

FORM/LANGUAGE

Answers are predictable to suggestive questions like the following: "Will you be fair and impartial?", "Do you believe a motorcycle rider has as much right to use the public highways as the operator of an automobile?", "If the court instructs you contrary to what you might prefer the law to be, will you follow the court's instructions?" Questions of this type are useful in obtaining commitment but are generally ineffective for obtaining information.

To learn a juror's real opinion, ask open-ended questions, such as: "What is your attitude regarding motorcycle riders on the public highway?", "What do you think about your ability to be fair and impartial in a case like this which involves a great deal of violence?"

When you inquire about highly critical areas, such as prior injuries, involvement in litigation, or undesired kinds of employment (insurance adjuster, police work, etc.) include in the question a reference to the members of the juror's family and his close friends.

Relate questions to everyday events when you can. For example, say to the juror, "The law says you must be convinced beyond a reasonable doubt and have an abiding conviction to a moral certainty before you find Mr. Brown guilty. Now this isn't the way we usually make up our minds in daily life. Will you follow the law and require the greater degree of proof called for by the law?"

DONT'S

Don't talk down to a juror or correct a juror's pronunciation. Avoid a "know-it-all" attitude. Don't display your brilliance.

Don't turn your back on a juror.

Don't allow your voice to sound cold, or monotonous. Cultivate variety and warmth of tone.

Never cross examine a juror or argue with him.

Avoid a tone of voice and manner which implies disbelief of a juror's response.

Don't allow yourself to appear irritated.

Don't risk embarrassing a juror by asking questions like the following which may display his ignorance and/or lack of education: "What college degrees do you hold?", "Do you attend church regularly?", "Do you believe a man charged with a crime has to show that he didn't do it?" (Many jurors will answer "yes" to this last question and will be embarrassed when you must point out they are wrong.)

Avoid questions carrying an implication of unfitness; for example, "Are you prejudiced?"

Avoid questions implying that a juror has not experienced the normal events of life, since such questions frequently kindle resentment; for example, "Have you ever ridden on a bus?", instead of "Mr. J, of course you have ridden on buses."

Unless it is necessary, don't ask questions that pry into such sensitive areas as religion, politics, and sexual experience. If it is necessary to touch on such matters, request the court to inquire into them.

Don't ask a critical question of a stupid person. You frequently will get the wrong answer.

If a juror gives an answer that shows he does not understand the question and probably never will, don't continue on to the point of embarrassing him, especially if you intend to excuse him.

Don't appear overly anxious while waiting for a response.

Don't repeat every educational question with every juror. Put a question or several, to two or three jurors and ask the others, either individually or as a group, if they've heard the question or questions and whether they would answer differently.

Never orally state an adverse opinion about a juror based on his race, employment, sex, etc.

Don't wear pins or rings reflecting memberships and/or beliefs.

MISCELLANEOUS

Rather than risk asking a juror questions that might be considered offensive, or getting answers which might have an adverse affect on other jurors, ask the judge to take on such questions.

An answer by a juror to a question about attitude may have an adverse effect on other jurors. On occasion it may be prudent to request, at the bench, permission to examine an individual juror out of the presence of the others so as not to contaminate the entire panel by a prejudicial answer. In practice, examination of a single juror outside of the presence of the other jurors is rarely requested or allowed.

Remember to ask whether jurors have had unpleasant experiences involving facts similar to those in the case being tried. Jurors are influenced by such similar experiences. Clearly differentiate between a juror's experience and the facts in the case to be decided. Likewise, if a juror has sat on another case, get a commitment from him that he will disregard any law learned in that case.

The language used and the connotation of words is important. In civil cases, for example, plaintiffs' counsel say "collision" and "corporation"; defense lawyers "accident" and "company." Defense counsel in criminal cases may attempt to depersonalize the opposition by referring to it as the "prosecution" or "the government," rather than "the People." By the same token, the prosecutor may attempt to depersonalize the defendant by consistently referring to him as "the defendant."

QUESTIONING TECHNIQUE

CONCERNING THE LAW

The court, in its discretion, can limit or prohibit counsels' attempts to indoctrinate jurors on propositions of law. Many judges prohibit any discussion of law beyond that of securing a commitment to follow the law as given by the court. Questions concerning the law tend to generate disputes among counsel and foster the preconditioning of jurors.

When the court allows it, use questions concerning the law to educate jurors relative to "burden of proof," "preponderance of the evidence," "negligence," "presumption of innocence," etc.

Questions of this type call for answers that are obvious and repetitious. To avoid boring repetition, do not direct all such questions to every juror.

Following are a few examples:

If the court instructs you that negligence is the doing of something a reasonably prudent person would not do, would you follow the instruction? And would you follow an instruction that it is not necessary for the defendant to act with extraordinary caution?"

"If the court instructs you that you are not permitted to find the defendant guilty on the basis of circumstantial evidence alone unless the proved circumstances not only are consistent with the theory that the defendant is guilty, but also cannot be reconciled with any other rational conclusion, will you have any reluctance about following such an instruction?"

Where the court forbids questions concerning the law, try a somewhat different tack which will allow you at least to touch upon the subject. For example, with respect to circumstantial evidence use an approach like this: "The judge will tell you what law you must follow in this case. A very complex part of the instructions will tell you about circumstantial evidence. Do you think you can keep from deciding this case until you hear about circumstantial evidence and all other instructions?"

SECURING COMMITMENT

To the extent that the court permits it, secure individual or group commitments where appropriate: for example, to not permit a difference in race and/or lifestyle between client and juror to influence a juror's thinking, to give your client a fair trial where the other party is charming and likeable and your client is not. Leading questions can be helpful. Commitments are often useful in final argument.

Examples of routine commitment questions follow:

"Will you follow the law, as given to you by the court, regardless of what you think it should be?"

"If a substantial verdict is justified by the law and the evidence, is there any reason you would not vote for it."

"If the plaintiff fails to prove his case according to the court's instructions, would you be willing to send him away with nothing even though he has been seriously hurt?"

"We all naturally have sympathy for Mr. Smith's terrible situation here, but despite that, will you decide the case on the facts and the law as given by the court, and not on the basis of sympathy?"

"Can you give a fair trial to John Smith, even though he has been convicted of a felony?"

"The people have the burden of proving their case beyond a reasonable doubt and to a moral certainty before you can find Mr. Brown guilty. This means several things. One is that the prosecution has to put its case on first and it might make things look pretty bad for my client. But you can't make up your mind then. Does that bother you? Do you realize that you can't come to a conclusion until all the evidence from both sides is in and the entire case is submitted to you? Will you promise to do that?"

"You realize that while you alone decide the facts, the final verdict can be rendered only in accordance with the law, and even though you hear all the facts you must wait until the judge tells you what the law is that applies in this case. Is that all right with you?"

"You will listen to all the evidence before forming any judgment, won't you?"

"Mr. J, you will voice your opinions during deliberations, and stand by your beliefs unless persuaded to the contrary, won't you, even though other jurors may disagree with you?" (As a prosecutor, however, do not secure commitments tending to militate against a unanimous verdict.)

Where a highly volatile matter is involved, be more painstaking in obtaining a commitment. In such situations (a) identify the attitude/bias; (b) speak kindly of those who have this attitude; (c) admit that the problem exists;

(d) confront the jurors by seeking an expression of opinion rather than a simple monosyllabic affirmation; (e) secure a commitment. For example: "I would be foolish if I didn't recognize that many people don't care for motorcycles and the people who drive them. Many of us have been offended by their noise and the appearance of some of those who ride them. In this case my client, Jim Smith, was driving a motorcycle when he was injured. Now my problem is this — someone may have such strong feelings about motorcyclists that he might find it difficult to be fair and impartial and return a verdict based solely on the law and the evidence. Mr. J, how do you feel about this?"

If the prospective juror gives an unsatisfactory answer, ask that he be excused for cause. If the answer is satisfactory, obtain a commitment. Say, for example, "Mr. J, if you are accepted, can I trust you to return a verdict based solely on the law and the evidence?"

Commitments are more effective than lectures that attempt to change deep-seated attitudes.

EDUCATIONAL/INDOCTRINATIONAL QUESTIONS

An indoctrination question — a statement in the form of a question — is a device for making educational statements about the case. The answer is predictable. Questions of this type are similar to those used in securing commitments, except that indoctrination questions are usually designed to be asked collectively, while commitment questions are more effectively used on an individual basis. The two categories tend to overlap. (It is not uncommon for judges to restrict or prohibit the use of indoctrinational questions.)

Examples follow:

"This is a civil suit. In a criminal case the prosecution must establish its proof beyond a reasonable doubt. In a civil case the rule is different; the plaintiff only has to prove his case by a preponderance or greater weight of the evidence. Now if the court instructs you on this matter as I have stated, will you follow the instructions of the court?"

"It is my duty to give my client the best possible representation. As a part of that responsibility I will make objections to evidence. We have rules in order to keep out unreliable evidence. It is my job to see that evidence of this kind is not admitted. When I object, will this cause any of you to be prejudiced against me? If you did become unhappy with me, would you hold this feeling against my client?"

"During the trial, I may make objections to the introduction of certain matters. I will do so in an effort to keep the trial within the framework of the rules of evidence. If I believe the rules are being violated and object, will this offend you? Will any of you allow the appearance, personality or conduct of any attorney to cause you either to favor or to be prejudiced against his client?"

"If you are selected as a juror, it is your duty to listen to the facts as they come from the witness stand and the law as given to you by the judge, and then decide the case solely on the law as applied to the facts in this case, and not the facts in some other case. Is there anyone who feels he or she cannot do this?"

"You are not required to lay aside your own experiences and common sense in evaluating the evidence. You are required, however, to determine the facts solely on the basis of the testimony and any other evidence produced in this case. Will all of you do that if selected as jurors?"

"As jurors it is up to you to determine where the truth lies. The judge will give you standards to apply in order to determine who is telling the truth. In weighing the evidence you may consider it in the light of your own experiences in life and your common sense. Will you do that? And will you wait until the case is over, until you have heard all the evidence and the instructions, before you make up your mind?"

"In this trial the jury will decide the facts and the judge will decide what law is applicable to the case. At the end of the case the judge will instruct you as to the law. Will you agree to follow that law?"

"You may not like or approve the law, but if you accept the responsibility of serving as a juror, you must follow it even though your idea of what the law ought to be is different from what the judge tells you it is. Is there anyone who feels he or she couldn't or wouldn't do this? Our laws and rules are made for us by our representatives in the Legislature and by our Appellate Courts. It is our duty to follow them even though we feel a particular law should be otherwise, even if we think it works a hardship on one of the parties to this action. Will all of you follow the law as given to you by the judge?"

"One of the instructions the judge is going to give you is that neither side has to produce all witnesses who have been shown by the testimony to have been present, or to produce any and all objects, documents, photographs or other things that are mentioned as being present in this case. Now, if we produce a minimum of evidence here, and you are satisfied from the evidence that the defendant is guilty, will you hesitate to bring in a guilty verdict because we didn't bring in all the witnesses who might have been present?"

LET JURORS TALK

Generally, questions that suggest the answer, such as "Do you have any prejudice against Mr. A?", tend to be meaningless so far as securing information is concerned.

Seldom does anyone admit to a prejudice. Getting a juror to talk is the best way to gauge his intelligence and his prejudices. Ask open-ended questions which encourage discussion. Give jurors time to move about in formulating their answers. Be warned, however, that open discussion can produce unexpected answers that may have a negative impact on other jurors and can embarrass self-conscious jurors who have difficulty in publicly expressing themselves. Consequently, many excellent trial lawyers avoid using open-ended questions. They believe the risks attendant to the free expression of opinion outweigh the advantages.

Examples of open-ended questions follow:

> "Mr. J, some folks are probably prejudiced against people who sue for damages for injuries they claim were caused by others' carelessness. How do you feel about this?" (Contrast this approach with such a question as this: "Do you have any feeling against a person who sues for the damages he claims were caused by another's carelessness?"
>
> "What opinions do you have about a lawsuit such as this?" (As contrasted with "Do you have any opinions about a lawsuit such as this?")

Oftentimes jurors are reluctant to speak candidly. To cope with any reluctance, humanize voir dire. Concede that, along with everyone else, you have prejudices. Give illustrations. They reassure that prejudice is a normal phenomenon, and the jurors will be less reluctant to talk about their own prejudices. A possible approach follows:

> "All of us have feelings and thoughts that tend to make us prejudge a person. I am no different, I sometimes prejudge people because their appearance or conduct reminds me of unpleasant experiences I have had. Such feelings are normal and not something we need be

ashamed of. I hope each of you will be honest with me and will respond without embarrassment as to your true opinions and beliefs''

Note: If you are satisfied with a juror, do not encourage him or her to talk. Something you or the juror says may result in a challenge by the other side. When you are satisfied, keep the questioning brief.

GENERAL QUESTIONS

General questions addressed to all jurors save time and avoid repetition. However, such matters as a juror's employment or residence, as well as his intelligence, cannot be learned from group questions.

General questions are useful in educating jurors and in obtaining routine information as to whether jurors (a) have been involved in accidents; (b) have been engaged in police or claims work; (c) have been sued; (d) are acquainted with litigants, witnesses, and attorneys; (e) have knowledge of the case; (f) drive an automobile; etc. Subsequent individual questioning, however, is likely to reveal that the group questions were not entirely effective in eliciting information. It is not unusual for a juror to divulge information in response to a personal question directed solely to him that was not forthcoming in response to a general question directed to the entire panel.

Group questions cause less resentment when potentially embarrassing or abrasive areas are probed than individual questions do.

Ask jurors to respond to general questions, either orally or by raising a hand. A risk incident to group questioning is that shy persons or those who fear being challenged may not respond.

EXAMPLE OF A GROUP INTERROGATION PROSECUTION/CRIMINAL

"Ladies and Gentlemen of the jury panel,

"This is a serious offense. A criminal charge has been levied against the defendant. Is there anybody here who has a special feeling of sympathy or pity for the defendant because he is charged with a serious offense? Are you willing to hear the evidence and decide the case based upon the evidence you hear, disregarding any feelings of sympathy or pity for the defendant?

"Is there anybody who has religious, moral, or philosophical qualms or misgivings about sitting in judgment of a fellow human being, for that is what you are going to be doing if you are selected? Does anybody have any reservations? It is a big responsibility. Does anybody prefer not to do that — not to sit in judgment on somebody else?

"The defense attorney raised the subject of presumption of innocence and reasonable doubt. Is there anybody here who believes there should be even more of a burden placed on the People than having to prove the defendant guilty beyond a reasonable doubt? Is everybody satisfied with that standard? Is there anybody who believes the People should have to prove the defendant guilty to an absolute certainty? Is there anybody who believes that is what the law should be? I take it by your silence everybody is willing to apply the law, and if the People prove the defendant guilty beyond a reasonable doubt that will be enough to convict him.

"Mr. J, you haven't sat on a jury case before. Do you understand what your responsibilities are as a juror? You will hear the evidence presented in the case. There may be conflicts in the evidence. It is your job to resolve those conflicts to the best of your ability. Do you understand that? Are you willing to take on the responsibility of trying to decide what happened, because that is essentially what your job is — to decide what happened on the date of the alleged offense, and after you have decided that, to apply the law the court gives to you?

"There are going to be several narcotics officers testifying in this case. Does anybody have the feeling or belief that being an undercover narcotics officer is kind of a sleazy sort of a thing for law enforcement officers to be engaged in? Nobody has any quarrel with the fact that sometimes police officers have to assume undercover roles, has he?

"I've mentioned the subject of narcotics officers in particular. Now I'll generalize a bit more. Have any of you had any experience with police officers — let's say a traffic violation that caused you to have a confrontation, so to speak, with a police officer? Has anybody had such an experience which developed into an unpleasant situation, for whatever reason, that might make it difficult for you to be fair and objective when listening to the testimony of police officer witnesses in this case? I take it nobody has had any particularly disagreeable experience with police officers when the officers have been active in the line of duty.

"Mr. J, if you were selected to remain on this panel and you were in jury deliberation where a vote was taken and the vote was eleven to one — it doesn't make any difference which way, and you were the one person not agreeing with the other jurors — at that point would you be willing to ask yourself: 'Why am I in disagreement with the other eleven members of the panel?' Would you be willing to ask yourself that question?

"Would you be willing to listen openly and freely to other jurors and discuss frankly with them the evidence presented? And, after freely and openly discussing the case, if you at that point realized that you had not considered some piece of evidence, or that you hadn't given enough weight to some piece of evidence; at that point would you be willing at least to reconsider your position? And if at that point you were convinced your earlier position was an erroneous position, would you be willing and able to change your mind?

"Do the rest of you believe you would answer similarly; that if you were convinced you hadn't considered all the evidence, you would be willing at least to reassess your position, and, if convinced differently, would be willing to change your minds?

"Has anybody, through friendships or acquaintances, developed any opinions about the court system in general or specifically about prosecutors?

"Is there anybody who believes that the defendant has more of a right to a fair trial than do the People of this state whom I represent? Does everybody agree that both sides have an equal right to a fair and impartial trial?

"The defense attorney asked a number of questions of you about your frame of mind, about placing yourself, so to speak, in the position of the defendant. Let me ask a similar question. If you were a deputy district attorney such as myself, and you were interested in a fair and impartial jury, a jury that could be fair and impartial to both sides, would you be satisfied in having somebody of your present frame of mind sitting on this case? Thank you."

CHALLENGE FOR CAUSE

Grounds for challenge for cause vary somewhat among the different states. Commonly recognized grounds follow:

The juror —

Is not a citizen.

Was a member of a jury which heard the same evidence in a previous case.

Has a suit pending against him.

Has an interest in the outcome of the case; for example, is a director or stockholder of a party or has an interest in an insurance company representing a party.

Has a relationship within prescribed degrees to a party in this case or his attorney.

Has a contractual relationship with a party; for example, is a partner, employee, employer, landlord, tenant, debtor, or creditor.

Has a friendly attitude toward a party or animosity against a party.

Has a bias, a state of mind with reference to the case or to any of the parties, which will prevent him from acting with entire impartiality and without prejudice to the substantive rights of either party.

Has preconceived opinions about the guilt or innocence of a defendant, against capital punishment, against conviction on circumstantial evidence, about the merits of the case.

Has knowledge of the facts of the case.

Within the categories above there are differences as to permissible inquiry. For example, in some states counsel may inquire about a juror's relationship with the defendant's liability insurance carrier. In others, inquiry is limited to interests in liability insurance carriers generally. Check the law of your state concerning challenges for cause. Challenges for cause are unlimited in number; peremptory challenges are not. Save your peremptory challenges whenever possible.

The extent to which you may examine jurors is usually left to the discretion of the trial court. Likewise, the removal of jurors for bias or prejudice is largely vested in the discretion of the court. By way of illustration, the mere fact that a juror once filed a claim for personal injuries is not in itself sufficient to disqualify him for cause. However, it might be. His description of that experience might directly or indirectly reveal bias or prejudice that would justify his removal for cause.

The ultimate test where bias and prejudice are concerned is whether a juror can follow the law and the evidence to the exclusion of other considerations.

If you want to retain a juror, don't agree too readily when your opponent asks you to stipulate to a challenge for cause. For example, your opponent may inquire in this manner: "Mr. J, I'm sure you can appreciate my concern about your business relationship with Mr. B and about how that might affect your ability to serve on this jury. Would you feel more comfortable if you were excused from this panel?" If the juror's answer does not indicate a strong feeling against serving and your opponent then asks you to stipulate to the juror being excused, politely decline, and ask the juror whether he would follow the law and the evidence, despite the relationship. Frequently his reply will eliminate any basis for a challenge for cause, thus forcing your opponent to use one of his peremptory challenges.

CHALLENGING TECHNIQUE

CHALLENGING FOR CAUSE

Generally, grounds for challenge for cause are readily apparent. If so, as counsel simply say, "It appears, your Honor, that Mr. J should be excused for cause." Technically the reason should be stated, but oftentimes this is self-evident. It is not unusual (a) for opposing counsel to volunteer a stipulation to the effect that the juror may be excused, or (b) for the court, recognizing the sometimes awkward implications for counsel, to inject itself and take the initiative where a prospective juror's answer indicates a possible basis for a challenge for cause.

In instances where there is a question about whether grounds exist for a challenge for cause, and where opposing counsel will not stipulate to excusing the juror ask to approach the bench. (The matter of obtaining a stipulation should always be discussed with opposing counsel privately and in advance before any request for a stipulation is made in open court.) At the bench, out of the panel's range of hearing, proceed as follows: "If the court please, the plaintiff challenges Mr. J for cause in that (state the reason) and asks the court to excuse him."

After hearing the position of opposing counsel, the court will either (a) excuse the juror, (b) refuse to excuse the juror, or (c) defer ruling until opposing counsel and/or the court conduct further interrogation. (In the latter instance you may request an additional opportunity to argue the matter after all questioning is concluded.)

If the court does not permit challenges for cause to be handled at the bench, you might wish to use phrasing such as the following: "If the court please, the plaintiff thanks and challenges Mr. J for cause in that (state the reason) and asks the court to excuse him."

Unless the court advises to the contrary, assume that you must make the challenge promptly upon discovery of cause. Otherwise, the court may deem the challenge to have been waived. (Note: In capital punishment cases you may find it expedient to voir dire the entire panel and then approach the bench to seek rulings on proposed challenges for cause.)

At the first opportunity after a juror is excused for cause or the challenge is overruled, commend the juror in question for his honesty and forthrightness and point out to other prospective jurors that the impanelment of impartial jurors is entirely dependent on honest and candid answers.

PEREMPTORY CHALLENGES

Suggested phrasing follows:

a. "If the court please, we thank and excuse Mr. J."

b. "If the court please, the defendant would like to thank and excuse Mr. J." Rather than: "I excuse Mr. J."

c. "If the court please, we thank and ask the court to excuse Mr. J." The latter phrasing is preferable because it tends to transfer some of the onus to the court. Always avoid "I excuse Mr. J."

If possible, avoid excusing a juror immediately after questioning him.

The majority of experienced trial lawyers never openly state a reason for exercising a peremptory challenge. However, a small minority of them believe that when you can do so without offending anyone, you should state a reason for the challenge.

Examples follow:

a. "I think, Mr. J, in view of your own accident experience, that we will excuse you;"

b. "I believe, Mr. J, that to save you any possible embarrassment, we will excuse you."

Whether you sit or stand while exercising a challenge is a matter of local custom, personal preference, or preference of the particular trial judge.

Always excuse jurors in a quiet, dignified way, whether for cause or by means of a peremptory challenge.

SAVING PEREMPTORIES

Develop cause for challenge by using leading and/or suggestive questions. For example, if a juror knows the other attorney, ask if he might be embarrassed or hesitant about returning a verdict against your client, or if he would prefer not to sit in order to avoid the possibility of any such embarrassment. A direct approach, such as, "Would you be biased?" is likely to get a negative response. An indirect approach is more likely to achieve the response you seek. You might ask, for example, "Am I correct in thinking it would be somewhat hard for you to sit under these particular circumstances? Wouldn't it be difficult, in all honesty, for you to give the plaintiff/defendant a completely fair trial under these circumstances?"

If you want to establish cause for challenge, ask questions that call for discussion about sensitive subjects; for example, "What is your attitude toward the defendant because he's been accused of a crime?", "What is the first thing that comes into your mind when you think of defense lawyers?" Discussions of subjects about which people tend to have unfavorable views may establish cause for challenge.

If a juror appears to be unsatisfactory to both sides, delay challenging in the hope that your opponent will excuse him first. If you do not reveal your inclination to challenge a juror, opposing counsel may excuse him, thus saving you a peremptory.

KEEPING A JUROR

Establish by your questions that the juror is a solid, responsible citizen. Your opponent may then realize that if he excuses the juror, his action may be perceived as being done because of race, age, sex, etc. This may deter him from doing so.

ACCEPTING WITHOUT VOIR DIRE

There are those who contend that if your opponent has questioned prospective jurors at length and the appearance of the remaining members of the panel indicates you are not like to improve your position you should consider accepting the jurors in the box without conducting any voir dire. The theory behind this is that it tends to convey the impression that you have great confidence in your case and the jurors.

An opposing view is that accepting a jury without questioning it implies disinterest or lack of confidence, and that you should always ask some questions, even if only a few of a non-controversial and/or educational nature. An overwhelming majority of successful trial lawyers adhere to the latter view.

EXHAUSTING CHALLENGES

Keep track of challenges. If your opponent is saving his and you are not, he may be able to alter drastically the composition of the jury after you have exhausted yours. Remember, passing a peremptory doesn't exhaust it. However, if both you and your opponent pass, you lose the opportunity for further challenge.

Carefully observe potential replacement jurors. If they don't appeal to you, exercise your challenges sparingly. Conversely, if potential replacements look good, exercise your challenges liberally.

GUIDELINES FOR CHALLENGING

Excuse any of the following:

a. A friend-of-the other-side, whether of attorney, client, or witness.

b. A resentful person.

c. One who is aware that you have unsuccessfully challenged him for cause.

d. One exhibiting antipathy for your client or a prospective witness for your side. For example: "I don't like policemen."

e. Anyone who would be seriously inconvenienced or suffer loss by serving.

f. Anyone with the same or a similar occupation as your opponent.

g. One who has voted "mistakenly" in a previous case.

h. Anyone whom you have challenged in a previous case.

i. An obvious leader unless there is good reason to believe he favors your side; otherwise, you risk, in effect, a "one man" jury.

j. Anyone you may have embarrassed or ridiculed.

k. Anyone who gives you bad "vibrations" even if you do not understand why.

l. Anyone with a strong commitment adverse to your position. For example, a teetotaler if your client is accused of being under the influence of alcohol.

m. Anyone you think will readily identify with the other side.

Follow the suggestions below consistently:

a. Be aware of the general nature of remaining prospective jurors; notice sex, age, clothing, race.

b. Take a look at what's left of the panel before exhausting your peremptory challenges. Otherwise, you may replace a marginal juror with someone more objectionable.

c. Consult with your client even if he is only a nominal party and the real client is an insurance company. He may have noticed something you missed. For example, clients sometimes perceive ethnic considerations attorneys may overlook. However, do not be unduly influenced by your client's opinions. Your client has neither experience in nor knowledge about selecting juries. Ask the court for a brief opportunity to confer with your client before exercising your right to challenge. Even if the client's opinion will not be determinative, it is still advisable to consult the client since it makes him feel he is part of the proceedings, and it impresses upon the jury the fact that the outcome of the case is important to him.

OBJECTIONS

Objections are generally deemed waived unless they are made promptly.

What is permissible often depends upon the attitude of the trial judge.

Theoretically, any question not related to a challenge for cause is objectionable. Courts, however, frequently give this rule a flexible interpretation. Bias/prejudice, a basis for challenge for cause, can be inquired into, and this inquiry generally provides ample guidance for exercising peremptory challenges.

All the following categories of questions are objectionable:

Those that attempt to instruct as to the law.

Those that misstate the law or the facts.

Those that argue the facts.

Those that are offensive.

Those that unduly invade a juror's privacy.

Those that ask a juror how he would conduct himself if certain problems arise during the jury's deliberations.

Those that attempt to condition a juror, that is, train a juror to a behavior pattern.

Those that concern a prospective juror's understanding of the law. (These are to be distinguished from questions about a juror's willingness to apply a principle of law, such as the presumption of innocence.)

Those which attempt to bind a juror in advance as to the weight he should give certain testimony or other evidence. (These are to be distinguished from questions about whether a juror would evaluate a particular witness by the same standards he would use to evaluate the other witnesses.)

Those that extract promises which in any way ask jurors to prejudge the evidence.

Appropriate phrasings for objections follow:

"I object on the ground that the question is not related to any ground for challenge for cause."

"I object on the ground that the question attempts to preinstruct jurors on the law."

"I object on the ground that the question does not correctly state the law."

"I object on the ground that the question asks jurors to prejudge the evidence." (It is improper to (a) ask for a commitment inconsistent with the jury's duty to hear all of the evidence with an open mind or (b) ask a juror to state his reaction to particular evidence or to give weight to the testimony of a particular witness.)

"I object on the ground that the question introduces inadmissible prejudicial matter. Further, I assign counsel's asking that question as misconduct and (a) request that prospective jurors be admonished to disregard it; or, (b) move to discharge the panel on the ground that the prejudicial effect of this misconduct makes a fair trial impossible." (Where opposing counsel has injected inadmissible prejudicial material and you want the panel discharged, it is better practice to ask to approach the bench before making your objection. Make sure the proceedings are not overheard by any of the prospective jurors.)

CAVEATS

Voir dire is the time you are most likely to bore the jury and the judge.

Don't expect to obtain a perfect jury.

Everyone is biased/prejudice in some way.

Jurors with even a little expertise in a field involved in the trial, for example, medicine, tend to dominate other jurors.

A single experience, such as a relative's being killed by a drunk driver, can prejudice a juror.

To avoid being excused, jurors often do not admit their biases/prejudices. On occasion, jurors lie.

Jurors, in complete good faith, may not recognize some of their own biases and prejudices.

An excused juror may be replaced by one equally as bad or worse.

Try to determine which jurors your opponent is likely to prefer.

People of high character follow instructions; people of low character follow their personal beliefs and prejudices.

Overly aggressive people have difficulty being impartial.

Bias/prejudice can either destroy or save your case.

Since social values are in a state of flux, you cannot always assume that a person from a particular group will think a certain way. For example, a banker's attitudes may be influenced by a beloved son who is a rock musician.

People who live in the city may have rural backgrounds which have molded their attitudes.

A juror may resent your challenge of his friend. (Note which jurors sit together in the courtroom. When a juror indicates by affirmative answers that he has had prior service in the present term, ask whether he has served in other trials with present prospective jurors. If he answers in the affirmative, seek their identification. In some instances you may want to inquire into the nature of the relationship; for example, whether they lunch together or socialize in the jury assembly room.)

If you embarrass a juror by inducing him to admit that he is unemployed, is on welfare, or has been convicted of a crime, you have probably incurred his animosity.

Annoyance at having to sit through what is perceived as an unnecessarily long trial can affect a juror's attitude.

It is wise to be leery of (a) jurors who are too anxious to serve or who are overly friendly, and (b) jurors who identify with your opponent.

It is wise to find out whether any juror has ever been a witness and the nature of that experience.

A juror's acquaintance with an attorney or witness may not be consequential; it depends on the circumstances. He may not, in fact, be a friend.

Those who have undergone suffering may either discount it or understand what it's all about.

Women who have had children generally do not get very concerned about mild or sporadic backaches and headaches.

Jurors generally do not identify with lawyers.

Jurors have anxiety about being questioned, and, possibly, embarrassed. It is sound practice to make an effort to relax them whenever possible.

If your client or any of your key witnesses mumbles, speaks indistinctly, or has a pronounced accent, be particularly alert for jurors with hearing problems.

If you are defending on liability, jurors may regard questions about damages as an implied admission of weakness.

A juror who voted to convict in a prior case where the evidence was very strong may be a good defense juror in a subsequent case where the People's case is weaker. Conversely, a juror who has voted to acquit on a weak prosecution case may vote to convict in a stronger subsequent case.

In medical malpractice cases it is wise for plaintiff's counsel to inquire whether jurors (a) have been employed in hospitals or in doctors' offices, (b) done charity work at a hospital, or (c) had past ambitions to become a doctor.

Keep in mind that such matters as concern for increased insurance rates or sympathy for a particular class of persons, such as landlords or doctors, often sway jurors' opinions.

Be careful of the following:

a. Inquiring too closely into the nature of a juror's work can embarrass the juror; for example, if he does menial labor.

b. Asking a woman how long she's been employed tends to reveal her age. Some women are very sensitive about age.

c. Asking some older men whether their wives are employed outside the home may touch a point about which they are sensitive. Consider prefacing your inquiry with such a question as "Many women today enjoy the challenge of working outside the home. Is Mrs. J one of these?"

d. Looking at a juror that you are privately discussing or allowing jurors to overhear a discussion of which they are the subject can trigger animosity toward you.

TACTICS

DEMEANOR OF COUNSEL

Be friendly and direct. Most lawyers prefer to stand reasonably close to the jury box but not so close as possibly to offend jurors; others use a podium. A minority, including some very successful advocates, prefer to sit.

It never hurts to be "the nicest guy in the courtroom", but don't fawn.

Project confidence in your side of the case.

GIVING THE IMPRESSION OF FAIRNESS

When you are satisfied that your opponent can successfully challenge for cause, offer to stipulate that the juror may be excused.

Seek to create an impression of fairness to both sides. Ask, for example, "Can you be fair to both the prosecution and John Jones in this case? You understand the People have a right to a fair trial also." This type of approach tends to enhance your credibility with the jury.

PLANTING SUGGESTIONS

When you ask a juror to overlook something that cannot be overlooked, you in fact emphasize an emotional factor while ostensibly attempting to do the opposite. Such a question as the following illustrates the point: "Will you ignore the fact that my client is blind and decide the case solely on the facts?"

AVOIDING BEING A BORE

Do not ask every juror every question. Question the first juror extensively, and thereafter, be selective in your interrogation. Inject new questions from time to time. Use an omnibus type of question to insure that nothing has been overlooked; for example, "Mr. J, you have heard the questions I asked the other jurors and the answers they gave, have you not? If I should ask you the same questions, excepting those involving personal experiences, would your answers be substantially the same?"

GETTING COMMITMENTS

Where you are allowed by the court, extract commitments — agreements — such as not to be prejudiced by negative information about your client; to decide the case solely on the law and the evidence. Then, if you remind jurors of commitments during argument, it is awkward for them to disregard the commitments.

NEUTRALIZING THE NEGATIVE

If you foresee making numerous objections, explain to jurors the reason (experience has proved certain kinds of evidence to be untrustworthy) for the rules of evidence and stress your obligation to invoke them on behalf of your client. Ask jurors not to hold this against your client.

Always bring out your problem areas with prospective jurors during voir dire. A few of the more common problems follow:

A client with unattractive speech and/or peculiarities in appearance.

A client with a bad personality — one who whines and is obnoxious.

A client who had consumed an alcoholic beverage.

A client who has made a previous claim for damages on account of a prior injury (if you represent the plaintiff).

A client who was a motorcyclist or a bicyclist at the time of the accident in question.

A client convicted of a felony. (Note: If many years have passed since the date of conviction, the jury may consider the other side unfair if it broaches the matter first. If this is your situation, consider the advisability of saying nothing.)

A case of medical over-treatment (if you represent the plaintiff).

Severe impeachment of a client.

An unappealing client vs. a charming opposing party.

An intellectually dull client vs. an intelligent opposing party.

Substantial injury vs. slight impact.

Subjective injury.

Sympathy for the other side.

These are a few of the problems which may produce a negative jury reaction. You will find representative questions designed to deal with some of them in those sections of this book setting forth suggested voir dire questions.

On occasion, before impanelment begins, you can eliminate some of these problem areas, such as improper impeachment, by making an appropriate motion heard in chambers outside the presence of prospective jurors.

When a juror gives an unexpected and injurious answer, such as "A motorcyclist takes his life in his hands when he drives one of those things", thank the juror for his frankness. Then tell him the court will define the rights and duties of all parties, including plaintiff/motorcyclist. Get a commitment that he will abide by the law, regardless of his personal opinion. Go a step further and get a commitment to the effect that if he is selected and some other juror expresses an opinion showing prejudice against motorcyclists that he will remind that juror he is in violation of his oath. Following this, get an admission from the other jurors that they are not prejudiced and have not been influenced by the remark. (Ordinarily, though, it is wise to excuse a juror making such a remark.)

Your objective is to ascertain whether a juror is capable of guaranteeing that justice will prevail over bias/prejudice. If you cannot obtain such a commitment from him, excuse the juror.

MISCELLANEOUS

If your opponent "dresses down," that is, pretends to be something he isn't, read a list of his partners and/or some of his well known clients and ask if jurors are acquainted with any of the former or have any present or past association with any of the latter.

If a juror is one who will probably be excused by your opponent — a claims adjustor by plaintiff's counsel, a safety supervisor by defendant's counsel — ask questions the answers to which will lead to a negative reaction among the remaining jurors when the juror is excused. For example, bring out that claims adjustors investigate accidents to determine who is responsible, that safety supervisors check to see that proper equipment is used and safety rules are followed.

Ask jurors about activities of theirs which may have a bearing on the case. For example, as counsel for the defendant in a street robbery inquire whether the jurors carry weapons, mace, whistles; or whether they walk with dogs as a means of self-protection.

In criminal cases, consider asking each juror to look at the defendant and then asking the juror if he presumes the defendant to be innocent as the law requires.

If you represent a corporation, have one of its representatives at the counsel table and use the words "we," "us," and "our company" to identify yourself with your client.

If a juror gives a negative response, restrain him from expanding on his views, since they may affect other jurors. If his response is inflammatory, thank him for his candor and establish that this is his own personal view which he wouldn't necessarily expect others to hold.

Jurors will reveal more if you call attention to such things as evasive answers, hesitancy, uncertainty in a voice, looking away, and other signs of nervousness. If you simply reassure them, you will discourage meaningful answers. On the other hand, you may alienate jurors if you cause them embarrassment.

Encourage weak jurors to speak up during deliberations and to be assertive about expressing their opinions. (This is not a good tactic, however, if you are seeking a unanimous verdict.)

Do not object to every question not perfect in form; to do so tends to antagonize jurors.

As a prosecutor in serious cases, make certain that jurors will follow the instruction not to consider the aspect of penalty or punishment.

SIZING UP JURORS

People do not always speak the truth, nor do they necessarily reflect the conventional attitudes of the group or race to which they belong. Their responses and background cannot always be accepted at face value. Some will say almost anything to become a part of the jury and others will say almost anything to get excused.

Most jurors want to serve and tend to say things they think will win approval. Some will lie. Generally, they want to appear bland, unopinionated, and inoffensive.

A juror's general promise to be fair is relatively meaningless.

Generalizations based solely on such factors as race, age, and occupation can be inaccurate when applied to a particular person. Many blacks, for example, are authoritarian and conservative.

An apparent attitude of friendliness or hostility towards a party or counsel is significant; however, the reaction of a juror to your case is more important than his reaction to you.

Occupation, economic status, and a juror's experiences or those of his immediate family as plaintiff or defendant are generally more influential than sex, race, age, or appearance. For example, a matron may have formed her attitudes earlier when living a fast-paced life. Be careful about accepting jurors who are in the same business or have the same occupation as an opposing party.

Urban jurors are generally more favorable to plaintiffs than rural jurors.

Intelligent, honorable, and responsible persons who have admitted to a bias/prejudice may well go more than "half way" to uphold their oath to be fair.

The way a juror says something — his intonation and facial expression — is usually more significant than the words he uses. How something is said can belie what is said.

A juror's hesitancy or evasiveness in answering a simple question can indicate thought, a reluctance to give you the answer you desire, or an inner conflict as to whether to tell the truth.

Differences in a juror's mode of response as between counsel suggests a disposition towards one side. On occasion a juror may attempt to ingratiate himself with a side he dislikes so as to avoid a challenge. Annoyance or resentment on the part of a juror towards you indicates that you probably need to challenge him.

The way a juror walks into the jury box and sits down may reveal something about him; for example, is he in pain; does he limp; is there any other indication of a prior injury; does he say "excuse me" (indicating concern for others), or does he ignore the other jurors?

A juror's response and conduct also may hold clues to his nature; for example, who does he look at when he answers; is he relaxed or rigid; is he nervous for no apparent reason; does he have difficulty in looking at the defendant in a criminal case; does he look away; does his tone of voice change; is he evasive, hostile, or resistant; does he look for support from the judge; does he pause inappropriately?

A fact, such as a close relationship with a police officer, outweighs a disclaimer to the effect that the fact will have no effect on the juror's verdict.

Answers like the following reveal doubts as to a juror's ability to be impartial: "I guess I can," "I hope I can be impartial," "I don't believe I am prejudiced," "I suppose I would do my best," "I'll try to abide by the court's instructions."

Jurors who visit with other jurors and smile are usually extroverts.

A woman's preference for Ms. oftentimes indicates an independent turn of mind and an open attitude about life and life styles.

It is reasonable to assume that it is difficult for a teetotaler to be objective about someone accused of being under the influence of liquor; that it is difficult for a man who works hard under adverse conditions to be sympathetic to an unemployed person seeking damages for a mild backache; that a retired pensioner seldom votes to award a large sum of money.

Jurors who are overly technical in answering questions and who question the wording of questions tend to be jury-hangers.

The reading material of a juror is an indication of his interests or attitudes.

A group of experienced trial lawyers rated the following factors in relative rank and order of importance:

1. Personal characteristics. (For example, has the individual suffered an injury or does he have an infirmity; is he intelligent, educated, strong-minded, etc., or is he the opposite of these?)
2. Occupation.
3. Personality.
4. Race.
5. Physical signs.
6. Nationality.
7. Body language.

8. Sex
9. Age.
10. Marital status.

These lawyers described the first four categories as "extremely important," the next five as "important," and the last, "marital status," as "of some consequence."

BIAS/PREJUDICE/FEAR

Keep in mind that everyone has some bias/prejudice, but that many will not acknowledge the fact. Bias/prejudice may be buried deep within the subconscious. It is a synthesis of many factors: the way we were raised; our racial, national, and cultural background; our education, age, economic status, religion, and marital status; and the impact of life's experiences.

General questions to a group about bias/prejudice will seldom elicit admissions.

Leading questions also reveal little about the existence of bias/prejudice.

Avoid asking a juror if he is "prejudiced"; you may rouse his resentment. Instead, inquire about his "feeling," "belief," or "opinion," rather than about his "prejudice."

Be aware that jurors tend to dislike motorcyclists, bicyclists, recent felons, hitchhikers, dope users, and welfare recipients.

Be alert to the fact that some jurors are prejudiced against people who file lawsuits; police officers (because of a personal experience, usually a traffic ticket); big corporations; particular corporations, such as, public utilities, oil companies.

In a relatively few criminal cases you may have to contend with strong community attitudes about the alleged crime and the defendant. If you represent the defendant, ask whether jurors have discussed the case with anyone, stated any opinions, or heard any opinions expressed. It is important to learn how jurors feel about the case and to determine what community pressures will be exerted against them if they vote for acquittal. Fear of being criticized for voting for acquittal may influence some.

When your client is a member of a minority group, you might ask a juror if that fact would influence his verdict. Beyond that inquire whether the juror has had experiences with members of that ethnic group which have given him a negative opinion of it. Be careful about asking a juror to openly state his opinion if it appears likely that it may tend to "contaminate" other jurors. Simply ask, without having him state them, whether he has strong feelings for or against your client, feelings which might influence him or cause him difficulty in being fair and impartial.

As appropriate, be sure to bring the following three problem areas into the open: (a) the sympathy felt for severely injured persons, (b) the belief that a defendant in a criminal case must have done something wrong, and (c) the belief that a defendant in a criminal case should prove his innocence, notwithstanding the presumption of innocence or the prosecution's burden of proof.

To cope with the problem of potential undue sympathy for the opposing party, repeat questions of the following nature several times with different jurors:

> "Mr. J, will you be loyal and faithful to your oath and return a verdict according to the evidence only?"
>
> "Can you render a just verdict without being influenced by your natural sympathies?"
>
> "If the court instructs you that the plaintiff has the burden of proving his case by a preponderance of the evidence, and if at the close of the case the evidence is equal on both sides, would you nevertheless vote for a verdict for the plaintiff because he is an elderly man who has been seriously injured and the defendant is a large company?"

"Mr. J, you'll not allow your natural sympathy for the plaintiff to influence you to vote against the defendant just because the defendant is a corporation, will you?"

To cope with the belief that a defendant is probably guilty of something, you might use the following approach when and to the extent it is appropriate:

Tell the jurors that you recognize it is a common belief that a defendant must have done what he is charged with but that the law presumes every person to be innocent until his guilt is proven beyond a reasonable dooubt. Ask if they can overcome their natural suspicion and begin the trial presuming the defendant to be innocent of the crime charged.

Ask whether they believe police officers are always right, never mistaken.

Ask whether they realize that criminal complaints are often filed on the basis of only one side's version.

Ask whether they realize that the police and the district attorney are not required to be convinced beyond a reasonable doubt before filing a criminal complaint.

Concede there is some evidence against the defendant, but point out that it is your contention it is less than the proof required by law, that is, beyond a reasonable doubt. Secure a commitment to withhold judgment until all the evidence is in and the court has given its instructions.

IDEAL JURORS

Ideal jurors are uncommon. Each juror's attitudes reflect a variety of factors, many of which tend to be conflicting in their impact. Jurors must be evaluated with respect to the nature of the litigants, the nature and complexity of the issues, and personal experiences of their own that are relevant to the case. For example, a person who has suffered an unfortunate personal medical experience is not a good defense juror in a medical malpractice case, regardless of what other qualities he may possess.

Follow the basic principle that you should like the juror and feel that the juror likes you. This is an instinctive, intuitive thing. The converse is also true; if you dislike someone or feel he dislikes you, regardless of the reason, be wary about accepting him.

Also, seek jurors who identify with your client, who tend to have similar characteristics.

Generally speaking, plaintiffs in civil cases and defendants in criminal cases want the same kind of jurors. Defendants in civil cases and the prosecution in criminal cases want the same type of jurors.

As you would expect, there is no unanimity among trial lawyers on this subject. Nevertheless, there is enough consensus to identify, in general terms, jurors who tend to take a particular side of a case.

PLAINTIFF/CIVIL

Lean toward choosing the following:

Inexperienced jurors.

Persons with an urban rather than a rural background.

Jurors whose sex is opposite that of the client.

Persons from racial minorities. (This is not a significant plus factor if the persons hold white collar positions.)

Emotional, warm, friendly, open-minded people who laugh.

Middle aged or young persons with long hair.

Liberals. (Note appearances.)

People with artistic occupations.

Blue collar workers or their wives.

Happily married persons.

Parents.

Relatively unskilled government workers.

Union activists.

Unemployed or downtrodden persons.

DEFENDANT/CIVIL

Lean toward choosing the following:

Experienced jurors.

Caucasians (WASPS).

Conservatives. (Note appearances.)

Persons engaged in a technical or precise occupation or trade, or in a profession.

Elderly or retired persons.

Physically and mentally tough individuals, those with stern countenances.

Childless persons.

Nonartistic individuals.

People who deal with claims and claimants (adjustors, doctors, nurses).

People who have witnessed a great deal of suffering.

Introspective people.

PROSECUTION/CRIMINAL (SEE ALSO DEFENDANT/CIVIL)

Lean toward choosing the following:

Persons with stable backgrounds.

Individuals from the same race as the victim.

Jurors who can mesh. (Be wary of two strong personalities.)

Those who are married and have united families.

Dominant personalities; people who supervise.

Wives, children and parents of policemen. (Beyond this it depends on the circumstances. People who know policemen realize that not all of them are infallible.)

DEFENDANT/CRIMINAL (SEE ALSO PLAINTIFF/CIVIL)

Lean toward choosing the following:

Persons nonconforming in appearance — the discontented and rebellious.

Where a child is the victim: caucasian females with experience in dealing with children of the same age and sex. (People without children sometimes place them on a pedestal, so to speak, insofar as credibility is concerned.)

A jury which reflects a cross-section of society.

Where a technical defense, such as entrapment, is to be used: intellectual rather than emotional persons.

THE FOREMAN

A strong foreman tends to dominate deliberations. As a rule, strong dogmatic foremen generally favor the defense in civil cases and the prosecution in criminal cases.

Jurors who often become foreman include the following types:

The born-leader type of person.

The juror who has had prior jury experience when the others have not.

The woman executive with or without prior jury experience.

The person whose employment involves supervisory responsibilities.

The tall man with a "distinguished" appearance.

The juror who says the right things and who appears overly eager to serve; he often maneuvers himself into a position of being nominated for the position of foreman.

The professional person.

The one black male juror among an otherwise all white jury, assuming he is over 35 years of age and employed.

The one male juror among an otherwise all female jury, regardless of whether he is a dominant person.

If you desire to "nominate" a foreman, use some such approach as "Mr. J, in your occupation you must make many decisions each day. Is that right? You hire and fire people? You preside over meetings? You are a leader of people? When you make decisions in your work, they are based on business judgment, are they not? You don't have to be convinced you are right beyond a reasonable doubt, do you? If you are selected as the leader of this jury, would you apply the reasonable doubt standard before you exercise your judgment?

In a civil case, after "business judgment" adapt the above thusly: "You don't have to be absolutely convinced you are right on the basis of legally admissible evidence, do you? If you are selected as the leader of this jury, in exercising your judgment you would rely only on the evidence introduced here in court and evaluate it in accordance with the law as given by the court, would you not?"

INFLUENCE OF OCCUPATION

A juror's affluence, position, and success ordinarily have a commensurate effect on the amount of damages the juror will approve.

A juror's occupation has great influence on his attitudes. Jurors are also affected by the occupations of their immediate family and close friends. A homemaker's attitudes, in particular, are influenced by her husband's occupation.

Sometimes it is wise to ask jurors about prior occupations. Often, a present position is one of recent origin.

People identify with those in similar occupations and also are aware of misstatements respecting the same.

A juror who might ordinarily be expected to favor one side of a case may not do so if the litigant in that position belongs to an occupational group which the juror dislikes.

An occupational group, such as construction workers, may be inclined to favor plaintiffs as to liability but tend to award lower verdicts than other occupational groups.

Retired people generally tend to be conservative.

Experts, and their spouses — doctors, nurses, engineers, for example — sometimes rely on their own experience rather than on the evidence. However, if your evidence coincides with the prevailing thinking in that field, such a juror can be a plus.

If your case involves technical matters, it might be wise to select at least one juror who can understand what is involved. However, it is probable that such a juror will exert an extraordinary amount of influence on jury deliberations.

People who give advice, for example, teachers and lawyers, tend to be opinionated and aggressive.

Successful people tend to be biased against the unemployed.

Longtime employees of a single employer tend to have great respect for authority.

Plaintiffs in civil cases and defendants in criminal cases should give favorable consideration to the following:

> Those with high and low incomes; the worldly wise; the artistic; blue collar workers; government employees; salespersons; office workers; the unemployed; executives, businessmen, and professionals who have liberal attitudes; the wealthy, insofar as damages are concerned.

Defendants in civil cases and the prosecution in criminal cases should give favorable consideration to the following:

> Those dealing in exact matters, for example, scientists, bankers, accountants; those who enforce discipline, for example, police officers, armed service officers; those who work in the insurance industry; investigators; nurses; doctors; businessmen; executives; professionals; landlords; farmers; teachers; engineers; technicians; pilots; those in middle income brackets.

INFLUENCE OF RACE/ NATIONALITY/RELIGION

RACE

Members of racial minorities tend to side with other members of that minority unless the latter are regarded as a discredit to the race. However, some members of racial minorities lean to the other side in order to prove their fairness.

Have-nots can be hostile to haves of their own race.

Blacks tend to be proplaintiff, prodefendant in criminal cases, and sympathetic to the "underdog," the young, the blue collar worker, and the unemployed. They tend to be prejudiced against executives.

Middle aged and younger Blacks tend to believe that the law and the police aren't always right.

Older members of minority groups tend to be conservative and prosecution-minded if they have had longtime stable careers.

Mexican-Americans tend to be passive.

People from minorities with relatively few members, such as Orientals, tend to go along with the majority.

Where the other party and a prospective juror are both members of the same minority group, some experienced lawyers recommend questioning about this relationship; others steer clear of the subject. Questions which might be used follow:

"Mr. J, does the fact that you are a Black and the defendant is a Black give him an advantage over my client, JP?"

"Would the fact that you belong to the same race as JP prevent you from deciding this case solely on the evidence and the law?"

"Can you assure us that if we accept you as a juror we will receive a fair trial from you?"

The importance of a juror's race with respect to his selection as a juror is declining.

NATIONALITY

People tend to favor those of the same national derivation as themselves.

There are both stern and compassionate people of every nationality.

The influence of nationality is decreasing as compared with its importance a generation ago.

Persons of the following races or nationalities tend to be proplaintiff in civil cases and prodefendant in criminal cases:

a. Particularly strong: Blacks, Irish, Italians, and Jews. Note: Jews and Orientals tend to be proprosecution in criminal cases involving serious violence.

b. Others: French, Greeks, Latins, Slavs (Hungarians, Yugoslavs, etc.), and Spaniards.

Persons of the following races or nationalities tend to be prodefendant in civil cases and proprosecution in criminal cases:

a. Particularly strong: Germans.

b. Others: Dutchmen, Englishmen, Japanese, Poles, Portuguese, Russians, Scots, and Scandinavians.

RELIGION

Religious fanatics are almost always self-righteous and narrow.

Devout church members tend to be conformists. However, some are very compassionate.

Jurors with a strong Catholic faith may favor Catholic litigants.

Religious bias is declining and is not a permissible area of inquiry except in rare instances.

INFLUENCE OF PERSONALITY/ PHYSICAL SIGNS/ BODY LANGUAGE/DRESS

PERSONALITY

Strong-willed people tend to be more open-minded than weak-willed persons.

Authoritarians, conformists, and rigid thinkers tend to convict in criminal cases and favor the defense in civil matters.

Jurors with low self-esteem are suggestible and tend to be dominated by stronger jurors.

Grouchy and irascible jurors tend to convict in criminal cases and to return defense verdicts in civil trials.

Happy people tend to favor plaintiffs in civil cases.

Extroverts tend to be liberal in awarding damages.

PHYSICAL SIGNS

Generally, it is not wise to attribute a definite meaning to a single gesture or movement. However, mannerisms can be revealing; for example, swallowing indicates that a question is unpleasant, a sigh suggests that the response was difficult.

Handicapped persons who have learned to cope with their disability are not as likely to be impressed with the seriousness of an injury as those who are not handicapped.

The reactions of a person who reacts to almost everything are of little significance.

Some short people tend subconsciously to resent tall persons.

BODY LANGUAGE

Trial lawyers appear to be divided on the credibility of "body language" as an aid in jury selection. The following guidelines are provided for those who give it credence:

Arms folded: somewhat antagonistic, not accepting what is said.

Fidgeting: impatient.

Talking through the teeth: hostile.

Woman with legs twisted in a knot: nervous.

Interlocked fingers with palms pushed out: unease.

Finger in the collar: discomfort.

Clenched fist: resistant or closed mind.

Pushing back and leaning away: negative reaction, even if outwardly agreeable.

Leaning forward: friendly, favorable.

Covering the mouth: uncertain.

Covering the entire face: unease.

Open legs: relaxed, friendly.

Swiveling of hips during answer: a negative sign.

Crossing the legs above the knees: resistant.

Crossing both legs and arms: greatly resistant.

DRESS

Flashy dresser: tends to resent authority; dress is an attempt to conceal an inferiority complex.

Immaculate dresser: tends to insist upon perfection in matters of proof; does not relate well to the average person.

A juror whose dress is atypical of his profession or business probably does not have the attitudes ordinarily associated with his profession or business.

Conservative dresser: tends to favor the prosecution in criminal cases and the defense in civil cases.

A juror who wears a lapel pin such as an American flag, a service club pin, chamber of commerce pin, lodge pin, etc. is generally conservative, favoring the prosecution in criminal cases and the defense in civil cases.

INFLUENCE OF PERSONAL CHARACTERISTICS

THE INJURED

People with a history of injury have a better understanding of pain and suffering than those who have never been injured. If a juror settled his own claim without a lawyer, he will tend to be conservative in awarding damages. If his case went to trial, he will tend to be prejudiced against defendants.

If a juror had an accident similar to the one in your case and was not injured he will tend to be skeptical, particularly with respect to soft tissue cases.

THE INTELLIGENT AND WELL EDUCATED

Jurors in this category can cope with the concept of a large verdict. They are desirable in cases where you intend to conduct a vigorous cross-examination and/or introduce strong impeaching evidence. They tend to be less biased in favor of their own ethnic or racial groups than those less well endowed. They also tend to be good prosecution jurors in criminal cases, unless the People's case depends on weak circumstantial evidence.

THE PHYSICALLY INFIRM

Jurors in this category tend to be opinionated. Some are sympathetic, some are sour; you must observe them carefully. If a juror has a serious infirmity he is not likely to get very excited about an injury that by comparison with his own condition appears to be minor.

THOSE WITH PRIOR JURY EXPERIENCE

Experienced jurors generally favor the defendants in civil cases and the prosecution in criminal cases.

Counsel for plaintiffs in civil cases should consider excusing jurors who have sat on cases involving substantially more serious injuries.

THE STRONG MINDED

Jurors in this category can be dangerous, for they tend to dominate, especially if they are males. Many experienced lawyers believe the risk inherent in retaining a dominate personality outweighs the potential benefit if there is any doubt at all about whether the juror will be favorable.

INFLUENCE OF AGE/ SEX/MARITAL STATUS

AGE

Mental age is more important than chronological age.

Physical faculties, memory, and attentiveness tend to diminish with age.

Older jurors generally are more tolerant of human frailty and more sympathetic to the injured than younger jurors. However, they tend to be conservative as to damages. They tend to have more respect for authority and more prejudices than younger jurors. They are inclined to be prejudiced against single persons and the young (except young children), and to identify with other elderly persons.

Among the elderly, those who have led successful (success can be in terms other than money), full lives are open-minded. Those with a narrow background and who are set in their ways are conservative and less sympathetic than others.

Young jurors tend to be tough-minded and unsympathetic to pain and suffering, yet more generous when satisfied as to the existence of real disability. They are optimistic about rehabilitation. They are inclined to be prejudiced against wealthy people, authority figures, and executives. Ordinarily, they are not very influential.

The young tend to be rash, unforgiving, and impulsive. It is not unusual for them to have difficulty in refraining until the end of the case from forming an opinion.

SEX

People tend to be less forgiving of their own than of the opposite sex.

Both sexes tend to be influenced by physically attractive members of the opposite sex.

Changes in society are tending to render obsolete much of the traditional thinking about females.

Women are often prejudiced against other women they envy, for example, those who are more attractive. This may be offset by an age difference between the client and the juror.

Women pay closer attention to details than men, especially where it concerns dress and appearance.

Women have more compassion than men for minorities, children, and young adults.

Women react more to pain and suffering than men and are generally more emotional and sympathetic.

Women are more likely than men to vote for the plaintiff.

Women are not more conservative than men with respect to awarding damages.

Women are not more unpredictable than men.

Women are more likely than men to convict when the crime involves forcible rape or a threat to a child.

Men are more tolerant of violence than women; for example, they accord greater weight to the right of self-defense.

Other things being equal, men are more influential than women.

MARITAL STATUS

Married people, particularly those who are parents, are generally better adjusted and more unselfish than those who are single. They are more tolerant of human failure. They tend to have more influence during jury deliberations than unmarried persons.

Parents tend to be favorable to children; at the same time, they are aware that children sometimes exaggerate and/or lie.

CHECKLIST OF QUESTIONS ON JURORS' BACKGROUND

The following list includes those matters customarily covered in voir dire. Not all of them are relevant to every case or to every juror. Some of this information can be obtained by asking general questions addressed to all jurors.

Occupation. (Include questions about spouse, adult children, and spouses of adult children.)

Residence. (Determine whether juror has always lived in the same kind of community, that is, rural or urban.)

Prior jury service. (Include questions about dates and whether service was civil, criminal, or both.)

Acquaintance with litigants, lawyers, witnesses.

Property ownership.

Any special education and/or training in law, medicine, nursing or other subjects involved in your case. (Include immediate family members *and* close friends within the scope of your inquiry.)

Involvement in police work or claims adjusting. (Include immediate family members *and* close friends within the scope of your inquiry.)

Prior injuries and complaints. If no claim was made for an injury or death resulting from an accident, as plaintiff's counsel ascertain why. (Include immediate family members within the scope of your inquiry.)

Involvement in claims and litigation of any kind, either as plaintiff or defendant. (Include immediate family members within the scope of your inquiry.)

Health: hearing, eyesight, sufficient stamina to serve through a lengthy trial.

Criminal cases only: inquire as to whether jurors have been victims or witnesses in criminal cases and the effect of that experience.

Operation of an automobile.

Use of services of medical doctors.

Belief in the reality of pain and suffering.

QUESTIONS: PLAINTIFF/CIVIL

These questions are comprehensive; they cover a variety of matters, not all of which are encompassed in every trial. Even of those that are relevant in a particular case, a majority of trial lawyers recommend that not every question be put to each prospective juror. Inserting new questions from time to time relieves tedium and helps maintain interest.

If the court and other counsel precede you, they may have asked some of the questions you were planning to use. Listen carefully so you will not be guilty of needless repetition. Critical matters at times require repetition in order to provide adequate emphasis.

The relative importance of specific information fluctuates from case to case. It is your responsibility to select questions that deal with the significant matters in your case, remembering at all times that an unduly prolonged examination is likely to be counterproductive.

On many occasions the answers you receive will necessitate your asking additional, follow-up questions.

PERSONAL INFORMATION

1. Where do you live Mr. J/Miss, Ms., Mrs. J? (Indicate that your question refers to the community rather than to a street address.)

2. Is there a Mrs. J/Mr. J?
3. What do you do for a living?/Are you employed outside the home: By whom are you employed?
4. How long have you been so employed?
5. What did you do before that?
6. Is Mrs. J employed outside the home?/What is your husband's occupation?
7. What does she do?
8. In the past, what other kinds of work has she/he done?
9. Do you have adult children?
10. What do they do? (If children are married, ask about occupations of their spouses.)
11. Have you served as a juror before? On what kinds of cases?
12. Do you own and/or drive an automobile?
13. Do you have any lawyers or doctors in your family? Among your close friends? (If the answer is yes, ask the nature of their practice; in particular, are they involved with claims.)
14. Do you know anyone who is employed as a claims adjustor?
15. Do you, or any members of your immediate family, have any training in law, medicine, or nursing?

KNOWLEDGE OF CASE AND PARTICIPANTS

16. Mr. J, do you know any of the parties involved in this case? Do you know Mr. A, the attorney for the defendant, or any member of his firm, the firm of A, B, and C? Do you know me or any member of my firm which, as you know, is the firm of D, E, and F?

17. Have you ever heard of this case before?

18. The witnesses who will be called to testify in this case are (read names). Are you acquainted with any of these people?

19. Are you acquainted with any employees of the defendant?

20. Is there anything about the nature of this case or about the parties involved that would make you hesitate to sit on this jury?

OTHER ACCIDENTS

20. Have you ever been involved in an accident?

21. Has anyone ever made a claim against you as the result of an accident or other situation?

22. Have you, or any members of your family, ever suffered injuries as a result of any kind of an accident? Was a claim made? Did you retain a lawyer to represent you? Tell us about it.

23. Was a lawsuit filed? If the answer is "no," ask: Do you have a feeling that you wouldn't bring an action for personal injuries no matter how serious the injury?

24. Was the case tried or was it disposed of in some other way?

25. Was it disposed of to your satisfaction?

26. Have you or your family been involved in any other lawsuits? Tell us about them.

27. Have you ever been a witness? Tell us about it.

BURDEN OF PROOF

28. You understand Mr. J, do you not, that each case must be decided upon its own facts and according to the law?

29. In criminal cases the requirement as to degree of proof is different from what it is in a civil case. In a criminal case the prosecution has the burden of proof. It must convince the jury beyond a reasonable doubt that the defendant is guilty. In a civil case the plaintiff has a lesser burden and need prove his case only by a preponderance of the evidence. Will you follow and apply the law in this case as the court instructs you, particularly as to the degree of proof?

30. Mr. J, as you know, the plaintiff must prove his case by a preponderance of evidence, which means merely that we must prove a better case than the case against us. That is what the law says we must do. Will you apply that law to this case?

DAMAGES

31. Do you have any quarrel with the law which permits a person to sue for legitimate compensation or damages for injuries and losses sustained through the fault of another?

32. How do you feel about awarding substantial damages where the proof and the law satisfy you that the plaintiff is entitled to them?

33. Do you believe in the reality of pain and suffering?

34. Do you feel that pain and suffering is of any less importance than purely financial losses? What is your attitude about giving damages for pain and suffering?

35. Would you cut the verdict just because, when its parts are added up, it seems like a lot of money?

36. On the basis of anything which you have read or heard about jury verdicts, would you have any reluctance about returning a fair and proper verdict, even if it was a very substantial amount?

37. Do you have a limit in your own mind of so many dollars, beyond which you wouldn't render a verdict, regardless of the evidence?

38. You understand, Mr. J, that if the plaintiff, JP, is not entitled to recover, he should receive nothing. On the other hand, if you find for JP, he is entitled to an award for the full amount of damages which he has sustained. The jury is not to compromise between the issues of liability and compensation. If selected, will you follow the law and be fair in this regard and "let the chips fall where they may"?

39. If we prove our case and you find that JP is entitled to your verdict and that his injuries are serious, will you award damages commensurate with the injuries and financial loss, even though that would require a verdict in a very substantial amount? (Where a large verdict is sought, always advise the jurors of that fact during voir dire.)

CONCLUDING

40. You heard, did you not, the questions I asked the other prospective jurors? Except for questions asking for personal information, would your answers be different in any way?

41. Mr. J, do you know of any reason I have not asked you about that you could not be a fair and impartial juror for both sides in this case?

42. Mr. J, if one of your family was the plaintiff in this case, do you believe he or she could obtain a fair trial from twelve jurors in your present frame of mind?

43. You understand, of course, that what both counsel for the defendant and I are seeking is twelve fair and impartial jurors to decide this case. Do you feel you can be one of those? Thank you, Mr. J.

QUESTIONS: DEFENDANT/CIVIL

These questions are comprehensive; they cover a variety of matters, not all of which are encompassed in every trial. Even of those that are relevant in a particular case, a majority of trail lawyers recommend that not every question be put to each prospective juror. Inserting new questions from time to time relieves tedium and helps maintain interest.

If the court and other counsel precede you, they may have asked some of the questions you were planning to use. Listen carefully so you will not be guilty of needless repetition. Critical matters at times require repetition in order to provide adequate emphasis.

The relative importance of specific information fluctuates from case to case. It is your responsibility to select questions that deal with the significant matters in your case, remembering at all times that an unduly prolonged examination is likely to be counterproductive.

On many occasions the answers you receive will necessitate your asking additional, follow-up questions.

PERSONAL INFORMATION

See questions 1-19 for Plaintiff/Civil. Additional questions follow:

1. Have you ever been involved in an accident case, either as a party or as a witness? (If a prospective juror answers "yes,", have him tell you about it.)
2. Do you drive an automobile?
3. Have you or any member of your family ever been hurt in an accident? Any deaths as the result of an accident? (If a juror answers "yes," get the details.)
4. Have you ever made a claim or sued anyone for damages arising out of any accident?
5. Did you retain an attorney? File a lawsuit?
6. Was the case tried in court? Settled?
7. Was the result to your satisfaction?
8. Are you acquainted with Dr. B (plaintiff's doctor)?
9. Have you or any member of your family been a patient of his?

ATTITUDE TOWARD DEFENDANT

10. Mr. J, you don't have any feeling against my client just because he has been sued in this case, do you?
11. As you sit there now, you don't have any feeling that JD is legally responsible for this accident or he would not have had this suit filed against him, do you? You realize, of course, that all anyone has to do to file a suit is to hand the papers to the clerk and pay a small filing fee. Then we have to come into court to defend ourselves whether we are liable or not.

12. In other words, Mr. J, unless the plaintiff offers sufficient evidence under the law to show that he is entitled to recover in this case you will not return a verdict in his favor, will you?

13. You understand, do you not, that the provision of the law requiring the plaintiff to prove his case by a preponderance of the evidence is a substantial one and is not merely a matter of words or formality?

14. If the plaintiff fails to prove his case by a preponderance of the evidence, you won't hesitate to return a verdict in our favor, will you?

15. Mr. J, what feeling do you have toward my client, JD, just because he's been sued?

PLAINTIFF'S BURDEN

16. You realize, of course, Mr. J, that a person may sustain an injury which is his own fault and that no one else may be liable, do you not?

17. I take it you understand, Mr. J, do you not, that it is not our duty to prove we are not liable in this case, but rather, it is the plaintiff's duty to prove that we are?

18. What do you think about the law which requires plaintiff to prove that the defendant was at fault? Does this seem fair?

19. Mr. J, the burden of proof in this case is on the plaintiff. Will you make him assume that burden?

FOLLOWING THE LAW

20. Will you follow the law as given you by the court in its instructions, even though your idea of what that law ought to be might differ from what it actually is?

21. Would you agree that it is our duty as good citizens to follow the law, even though we might like to change it?

22. And you will follow that law despite any feeling of sympathy you might feel for either of the parties here, won't you? In other words, will you be willing to "let the chips fall where they may"?

SYMPATHY

23. Of course, you know, Mr. J, do you not, that sympathy has no place in deciding the issues of a case such as this?

24. It is natural for all of us to have a feeling of sympathy for anyone who has been injured. However, you would not take money from us and turn it over to the plaintiff just because you might have a feeling of sympathy for him, would you?

25. Will you try to keep your feelings of sympathy from preventing you from doing your duty as a juror? Will you return a verdict based only on the law and the evidence?

26. When you hear the evidence in this case I'm sure you will share the same natural feelings of sympathy that all of us have, including JD and myself, for the situation this plaintiff is in. Nevertheless, will you be able to put aside these normal feelings of sympathy and decide this case solely on the evidence and the law as the judge states it?

KEEPING AN OPEN MIND

27. The plaintiff has an obligation to present the evidence he wishes. After he gets through, we present our evidence. Will you keep an open mind until you

have heard all of the witnesses before you make up your mind as to who is right and who is wrong?

28. Will you give due consideration to any and all defenses which the court permits us to offer?

ATTITUDE TOWARD CORPORATIONS

29. Will you give both sides here a fair and impartial trial, Mr. J, even though the plaintiff is an individual and my client is a corporation? After all, a corporation is made up of people just like all of us here in the courtroom.
30. You feel, do you not, that my client is entitled to a fair hearing in this case?
31. Would you require less proof against us because we are a company?
32. I take it also you understand that the question of whether we are liable is one question and the amount of plaintiff's damages is another question?
33. If the evidence justifies it, could you find a verdict for us just as readily as you could find a verdict for the plaintiff?

RULES OF EVIDENCE

34. Now, Mr. J, you understand, of course, that cases are tried and governed by rules, just as everything else in life is, do you not?
35. You also understand, do you not, that these rules tell us what evidence is admissible in the trial of cases?
36. If it should become necessary for either the attorney for the plaintiff or me to make objections to certain evidence offered, you will understand, will you not,

that we, in objecting, feel the evidence being offered is not admissible according to the rules and believe it is our duty to object? If either of us should make such objections during the trial of this case, you won't hold that against either of us or our clients, will you?

CONCLUDING

37. You heard the questions, did you not, that I asked the other prospective jurors? Except for those questions calling for personal information, would your answers be any different?
38. Mr. J, do you know of any reason why you might tend to be prejudiced in this case?
39. If you were being sued, would you want someone to decide your case who was in the same frame of mind you are in right now?
40. Then you feel you can give both sides a fair and impartial trial and render a just verdict between us? Thank you, Mr. J.

QUESTIONS: PROSECUTION/CRIMINAL

These questions are comprehensive; they cover a variety of matters, not all of which are encompassed in every trial. Even of those that are relevant in a particular case, a majority of trial lawyers recommend that not every question be put to each prospective juror. Inserting new questions from time to time relieves tedium and helps maintain interest.

If the court and other counsel precede you, they may have asked some of the questions you were planning to use. Listen carefully so that you will not be guilty of needless repetition. Critical matters at times require repetition in order to provide adequate emphasis.

The relative importance of specific information fluctuates from case to case. It is your responsibility to select questions that deal with the significant matters in your case, remembering at all times that an unduly prolonged examination is likely to be counterproductive.

On many occasions the answers you receive will necessitate your asking additional, follow-up questions.

PERSONAL INFORMATION

1. Where do you live Mr./Miss, Ms., Mrs. J? (Indicate that your question refers to the community rather than to a street address.)

2. Is there a Mrs. J/Mr. J?
3. What do you do for a living? Are you employed outside the home? By whom are you employed?
4. How long have you been so employed?
5. What did you do before that?
6. Is Mrs. J employed outside the home? / What is your husband's occupation?
7. What does she do?
8. In the past what other kinds of work has she/he done?
9. Do you have adult children?
10. What do they do? (If children are married, ask about occupations of their spouses.)
11. Have you served as a juror before? On what kinds of cases?
12. Have you, or any members of your family or close friends, ever been a defendant in a criminal case?
13. Do you know the defendant or anyone in any way associated with him?
14. Do you know Mr. A who represents the defendant?
15. Do you know anyone sitting on our side of the table?
16. Do you know any of the persons whose names I previously read who may be called as witnesses?

COMMITMENT TO FAIR TRIAL

17. You understand, do you not, that a criminal trial is a search for the truth, not a personality contest between opposing counsel?
18. The defendant is entitled to a fair trial. Can you give him one?

19. The People also are entitled to have twelve open minded jurors who are fair, unprejudiced, and unbiased. Isn't that right?

20. Do you feel as you sit here now that you can be that type of juror?

THE PEOPLE'S BURDEN

21. You understand the People have the duty of proving the defendant guilty beyond a reasonable doubt? Reasonable doubt means simply that — not just any doubt — but doubt based on reason.

22. You understand, do you not, that if from all the evidence in the case we meet our burden of proof, then it would be your duty to return a verdict finding this defendant guilty?

23. If the vote in the jury room should be eleven against your one, would you ask yourself whether your position is really reasonable in light of the position of eleven other reasonable people?

24. Do you understand that if the People prove this defendant guilty as the law requires, the only way you can fulfill your duty as a juror and your oath as a juror is by voting for a guilty verdict?

ACCOMPLICE

25. An accomplice is a person who testifies to his participation in a crime and also testifies to the participation of others in that crime. Will that fact alone cause you to be prejudiced or biased against such a witness?

26. Would the fact that a witness is an accomplice cause you arbitrarily to reject his testimony?

27. If the court tells you at the close of all the evidence that the testimony of an accomplice should be regarded with distrust and acted upon with caution, will that cause you automatically to reject the testimony of that accomplice?

28. If the court instructs you that the testimony of an accomplice is competent legal evidence, will you consider it?

29. If you feel you would be prejudiced or biased because Mr. W is an accomplice, you will tell us so now, won't you?

30. You understand, do you not, that it is only important whether you believe the accomplice, not whether you like or admire him? Can you keep this distinction in mind?

MISCELLANEOUS

31. All possible defendants may not be on trial here. Will you promise that you will not speculate about the reason for the absence of a possible defendant?

32. As a trier of fact, will you promise in evaluating the testimony of a witness to consider the interest of that witness in the outcome of the trial?

33. You have probably heard the saying, "To err is human, to forgive, divine." As a juror it is not within your responsibilities to forgive or excuse. You understand, do you not, that your sole duty is to determine the question of guilt or innocence?

34. If you are selected as a juror in this case, it will be your duty to listen to all the evidence in the case and then determine the credibility of all witnesses, according to standards the court will give you. Are you willing to do that?

35. Are you capable of evaluating the evidence without being affected by passion or prejudice?

36. Are you capable of considering the evidence alone without any consideration of penalty or punishment?

37. You heard the questions I asked the other prospective jurors, did you not? Except for answers to personal questions, would your answers be different in any way?

38. Mr. J, do you know of any reason which has not been discussed that leads you to believe you may not be able to be a fair and impartial juror in this case?

39. You understand, of course, that both counsel are seeking twelve fair and impartial jurors to decide this case. Do you feel you can be one of those? Thank you, Mr. J.

QUESTIONS: DEFENDANT/CRIMINAL

These questions are comprehensive; they cover a variety of matters, not all of which are encompassed in every trial. Even of those that are relevant in a particular case, a majority of trial lawyers recommend that not every question be put to each prospective juror. Inserting new questions from time to time relieves tedium and helps maintain interest.

If the court and other counsel precede you, they may have asked some of the questions you were planning to use. Listen carefully so that you will not be guilty of needless repetition. Critical matters at times require repetition in order to provide adequate emphasis.

The relative importance of specific information fluctuates from case to case. It is your responsibility to select questions that deal with significant matters in your case, remembering at all times that an unduly prolonged examination is likely to be counterproductive.

On many occasions the answers you receive will necessitate the asking of additional, follow-up questions.

PERSONAL INFORMATION

1. Where do you live Mr./Miss, Ms., Mrs. J? (Indicate that your questions refers to the community rather than to a street address.)
2. Is there a Mrs. J/Mr. J?
3. What do you do for a living? / Are you employed outside the home? By whom are you employed?
4. How long have you been so employed?
5. What did you do before that?
6. Is Mrs. J employed outside the home? / What is your husband's occupation?
7. What does she do?
8. In the past what other kinds of work has she/he done?
9. Do you have adult children?
10. What do they do? (If children are married, ask about occupations of their spouses.)
11. Have you served as a juror before? On what kinds of cases?
12. Was there anything about your previous jury experience that would lead you to feel you mayhave some bias either for the prosecution or against the prosecution?
13. Is there anything about the nature of the charges contained in the information that would prevent your considering this case fairly and impartially?

14. Have you, or a relative or close friend of yours, ever been the victim of a crime? When? What type of crime?
15. Was the offense prosecuted? What was the result?
16. Have you, a relative or a close friend, ever been the complaining witness in a criminal prosecution?
17. Do you belong to any organization which has for its purpose the suppression of crime?
18. Have you or any of your close friends or relatives ever been engaged in public or private law enforcement work at any time, either as a paid employee or as a volunteer?
19. Have you ever studied law?
20. Are you personally acquainted with the District Attorney or any deputies in his office, including Mr. C who is trying this case?
21. Do you know any of the persons whose names you have heard read and who may be called as witnesses in this case?
22. Do you know anything about the facts of this case except what you have heard in court today?

ATTITUDE TOWARD DEFENDANT

23. Mr. J, do you have any feeling against my client, JD, because he has been accused of a crime?
24. Do you feel he's guilty simply because a complaint has been filed against him? Or because he is in custody? (Give a brief explanation of the bail system if appropriate, that is, if your client is in custody.)
25. Does the fact that JD is charged with more than one count cause you to feel he is more likely to be

guilty than if he were charged with only one count? Would you require less proof than otherwise to convict because there are multiple counts?

A PUBLICIZED CASE

26. Have you read any newspaper accounts of this case? What newspapers?
27. What have you read about this case in the newspapers or heard about it on television or radio?
28. Would you consider this case differently from a case which had not been in the public attention?
29. Have you formed any opinion as to the guilt or innocence of JD?
30. If you have formed, or heard others express, an opinion regarding this case, would it take evidence to change that opinion or remove from your mind what you have heard?
31. Knowing what you do about this case and the opinion you have formed about it, would you be entirely satisfied to be tried by a jury in your present frame of mind if you were the person charged with this offense?
32. Would you render a verdict in this case according to the law and the evidence and not allow the fear of criticism from any source to influence your verdict?
33. Would you be uncomfortable around your neighbors or fellow workers if you voted for an acquittal in this case?
34. If you are sworn as a juror, will you lay aside any opinion you may now have and act solely upon the evidence introduced here and upon the instructions of the court?

KEEPING AN OPEN MIND

35. In this case, Mr. P, the prosecutor, must present his evidence first. When he is through, if we desire to do so, we have the right to present our evidence. Will you promise to keep an open mind until you have heard all of the evidence before you formulate any opinion on the issue of innocence or guilt?

ATTITUDE TOWARD POLICE OFFICERS

36. If police officers testify, will you apply the same standards in evaluating their testimony as you would in evaluating that of any other witness?

37. You realize that people witnessing the same event may see it differently. It is for the jury to determine how much weight is to be given a witness's testimony. Will you test the credibility of witnesses in accordance with the rules of law? And in light of your own past experience? Would you give more credence to the testimony of a police officer simply by reason of the fact that he is a policeman than to the testimony of any other person? Do you agree that it is possible a police officer might not tell the truth?

FOLLOWING THE LAW

38. You realize, do you not, that it is our duty as good citizens to obey the law even though we may think the law should be different from what it actually is? Even if we think the law is unwise?

39. The law places a substantial burden of proof upon the prosecution. Mr. J, will you make the prosecutor meet that burden of proving his case beyond all reasonable doubt?

40. Will you view the evidence in the light of your own experience and in accordance with the instructions of the court and then make up your mind as to where the truth lies?

41. You are aware, are you not, that you cannot consider your personal opinion about any facts not proven as a basis for your verdict?

42. You realize, do you not, that you may believe as individuals that certain facts exist, but that as jurors you can act only upon the evidence introduced in the trial of this case, and that from those facts and those facts only you must arrive at your verdict?

PRESUMPTION OF INNOCENCE/ BURDEN ON PROSECUTION

43. You understand, do you not, that while in a civil case a party need only prove his case by a mere preponderance of the evidence, in a criminal case it is necessary for the prosecution to prove the defendant guilty beyond a reasonable doubt — that is, to a moral certainty?

44. As you also know, JD is presumed to be innocent until such time as the prosecution may prove him guilty beyond a reasonable doubt. How do you feel about that?

45. You realize, do you not, that a complaint is merely an accusation and is not evidence which you may use in determining guilt or innocence?

46. Do you think it possible that because of suspicious circumstances an innocent person may be charged with a crime?

47. The law presumes a defendant to be innocent until he is found guilty. Do you believe in that principle of law strongly enough to vote for acquittal unless you are satisfied of JD's guilt beyond a reasonable doubt?

48. Do you agree with our principle of law that a defendant in a criminal case may not be convicted unless the jury is convinced that he is guilty beyond a reasonable doubt — to a moral certainty — of the truth of the charge?

49. Mr. J, if the evidence showed two reasonable theories as to what happened, one pointing to guilt and the other to innocence, and the judge told you that in such a situation you should return a verdict of not guilty, would you follow the law in that respect? How does that seem to you? Is it fair?

50. If the judge instructs you that the crime charged includes several elements, will you vote for acquittal unless you are satisfied that the proof establishes all of the elements?

51. You understand, do you not, it is not our responsibility to prove that JD is innocent?

52. You understand, do you not, that the burden of proof is always on the prosecution, and that the defendant is under no obligation to present any evidence in his behalf?

53. Do we have your promise that you would not return a verdict of guilty on mere suspicion, however great?

54. If you have a reasonable doubt as to JD's guilt, is there any reason you would not vote for an acquittal?

MULTIPLE DEFENDANTS

55. Do you believe in guilt by association?

56. Do you believe that if a person is charged with a crime along with others, and one of them is proved to be guilty, all of them must be guilty?

57. Do you understand that you must decide separately the guilt or innocence of each defendant?

PREJUDICE

58. Can you be fair and impartial toward persons whose life-styles differ considerably from your own?

59. Do you have any male children? Do they have long hair or wear what you consider to be unorthodox clothing?

60. How do you feel about people whose personal appearance, clothing, and general life-style are different from those of most Americans?

61. Would the fact that JD was once convicted of a criminal offense cause you to prejudge him or to totally disregard his testimony?

62. The judge will tell you that you may use JD's prior record only in the matter of assessing his credibility; but, despite what the judge tells you, would you nevertheless feel, because of his record alone, that JD is more likely than otherwise to have committed this crime with which he is charged?

63. You and JD appear to be of the same race. Does that make any difference in your attitude or in your ability to give both sides a fair trial? / You and JD are of different races. Will that affect your ability to be a fair and impartial juror?

64. Would you be influenced in your verdict in this case just because crime in the United States is generally a serious problem?

DEFENDANT'S TESTIMONY

65. If JD testifies, will you weigh his testimony by the same standards you apply to that of other witnesses?
66. Do you feel that some special qualification or limitation should be placed on JD's testimony? He is on trial. Would that cause you to judge his testimony by standards different from those by which you will judge other testimony?
67. Would you give more credence to the testimony of a white person than you would to that of a black person because of the difference in race?
68. Would you give less weight to the testimony of a witness called by the defense than you would to the testimony of a witness called by the prosecution by reason of that fact alone?

SILENT DEFENDANT

69. Do you understand that JD need not testify if he chooses not to. The decision as to whether a defendant testifies is left to the defendant, acting with the advice of his attorney. If he chooses not to testify, will this lead you to think he is guilty?
70. Would it be necessary for JD to testify for you to find him not guilty?

INVOLVEMENT OF VIOLENCE

71. Will the fact that there may be gruesome descriptions of injuries affect your ability to be fair and impartial? Will you become carried away by anger?

72. Because this case involves violence, do you feel you might require less proof than in a case which did not involve violence? Would you give JD the same fair trial you would had he been charged with a nonviolent offense?

RULES OF EVIDENCE

73. Now, if it should become necessary for either the attorney for the People or me to object to certain offered evidence, you will understand, will you not, that we, in objecting, feel the evidence being offered is not admissible according to the rules of evidence and believe it is our duty to object? If I make objections to evidence, will you hold it against the defendant?

ATTITUDE TOWARD LAWYERS

74. Would you give added weight to the arguments of the prosecutor because he bears the impressive title of "district attorney"?

75. Does the fact that the prosecution has been brought in the name of the People of this state add righteousness to the prosecution in your mind?

76. You realize, do you not, that the district attorney and I are both doing our best to represent our clients?

COMMITMENT TO OWN VERDICT

77. If you have a reasonable doubt about my client's guilt, and, after listening to the arguments of your fellow jurors, still have that reasonable doubt, will you stand by your belief and refuse to change your verdict, even though it might result in a mistrial? You realize, of course, that there is such a thing as a hung jury?

78. You realize, do you not, you are doing your duty as a juror by acquitting the defendant if you are not convinced of his guilt beyond a reasonable doubt?

79. Do you believe your decision in this case would be influenced by what your friends or neighbors might think concerning the case?

80. Would the inconvenience of having to spend a night or nights away from your home prevent you from following your own conviction about this case if you had a reasonable doubt about the guilt of the defendant?

81. Would you change your position solely because the other eleven jurors took a different position?

82. If you are chosen as a juror in this case, will you stand on your own individual analysis of the evidence and on your own individual judgment regardless of pressure, emotional outbursts of other jurors, or angry remarks other jurors may direct to you?

CONCLUDING

83. Assuming that a loved one of yours were on trial here today instead of JD, would you feel satisfied to have twelve jurors hear the case if they were in the same frame of mind as you presently are?

84. Would you give JD the benefit of your individual opinion and vote for a verdict of not guilty as long as you have a reasonable doubt of his guilt, even though the other eleven jurors voted the other way?

85. Do you know of any reason you could not serve in this case as a fair and impartial juror? Thank you, Mr. J.

QUESTIONS FOR SPECIAL SITUATIONS

DRUNK DRIVING: CRIMINAL PROSECUTION

1. Do you drink on social occasions?
2. Do you object to others taking a social drink?
3. Have you ever been a member or supporter of any group that seeks to prohibit the sale or use of alcoholic beverages?
4. Do you feel that one who drinks alcohol and then drives a car has violated the law, regardless of the amount he consumed or its effect on him?

5. You realize, do you not, it is not unlawful to drive a car after taking a drink of alcohol, as long as the alcohol does not affect the ability of the driver to operate his automobile as an ordinary reasonable person?
6. You would not find my client guilty simply because he drank and then drove a car, would you?
7. Could you regard a test result as just one piece of evidence to be weighed with all the other evidence?
8. You wouldn't automatically let a machine convict my client, JD, would you, Mr. J?

CLIENT DRINKING: CIVIL CASE

1. Do you occasionally take a social drink?
2. Mr. J, the evidence will disclose that JP had one or two or even three drinks shortly before this accident. Will that fact alone cause you to vote against him?
3. Have you ever expressed your opinion about people who drink and drive?
4. Mr. J, would you please tell me your thoughts about drinking and driving?
5. How do you feel about a person's driving a vehicle after having taken a drink or two?
6. Do you believe you could listen to the evidence to determine whether the drinks JP took had anything to do with the cause of the accident?
7. And if they did, I guess you could vote against JP, couldn't you?
8. And if they didn't, and if the evidence and law supported a verdict in his favor, would you vote accordingly?

9. It is extremely important that you carefully consider whether you will be consciously or subconsciously prejudiced against JP for having had those drinks. Is there anything about that fact which makes you feel you can't objectively listen to the evidence in this case?

TO RETAIN AN ACQUAINTANCE

1. Mr. J, you and I have been previously acquainted for some time, is that not true?
2. I suppose a man of your position is acquainted with a number of attorneys.
3. I have never represented you, have I?
4. As a fair man, Mr. J, would you let your acquaintanceship with me or any other attorney influence your decision in this case?
5. You would decide the issues on the merits and under the instructions given to you by the judge. That is true, is it not?

REVEALING A NEGATIVE FACT/ SECURING A COMMITMENT

1. Now, Mr. J, JD was convicted of robbery some years ago. Does this fact cause you to feel you could not impartially and fairly serve as a juror on this case?
2. Do you feel that in spite of what I've just told you, you can hear the evidence with an open and unbiased mind?
3. In other words, as you sit here now, you believe, do you not, that you can decide the issues in this case regardless of any facts outside this case?

4. I'm not asking you to condone or even forgive JD for the previous crime he committed, but can you assure me that he will receive a fair and impartial trial in your hands in the present case?
5. In other words, you are going to reach your verdict only on the facts in this case, are you not?
6. Am I correct in believing that if any juror violated his promise under oath and attempted to influence you against JD because of his past misconduct, you would ignore such an attempt?
7. And, once again, can you assure us that if we accept you as a juror in this case, you will give everyone a fair trial?

COPING WITH PREJUDICE

1. The evidence will establish that JP was driving a motorcycle. I suppose many of us are somewhat prejudiced against motorcycles. Am I right?
2. Admittedly, it may be difficult for most people to give a motorcycle driver a fair trial, and yet that's exactly what you must do. Do you feel you can give my client, JP, a fair trial?
3. Certainly, we all agree that a motorcyclist should observe the traffic laws, just as the driver of an automobile should. By the same token, while the driver of a motorcycle owes a duty of care to other motorists not to injure them, the driver of an automobile owes the same degree of care to a motorcycle driver. Isn't that right?
4. You don't feel that the driver of a car has any special privileges because the other person is driving a motorcycle, do you?

5. You don't believe that simply because one of the parties to a collision was driving a motorcycle he was at fault by reason of that fact alone, do you?
6. If the evidence proves that JP was careful while driving his motorcycle and that this collision was caused by the carelessness of the defendant, would you have any hesitancy in finding in JP's favor?
7. Will you decide this case as impartially as you would a case where two cars were involved instead of one car and one motorcycle?
8. Will you assure me that if you are selected to serve in this case, JP will receive a fair trial?

COUNTERING A COMMITMENT

1. You have told Mr. X that you will give his client a fair trial. Now, in your effort to be fair, I trust you are not going to lean so far in his direction that you will not be fair to my client, JD. You won't do that, will you?
2. The defendant is entitled to exactly the same consideration that you give the plaintiff. Will you call it exactly as you see it, regardless of any other consideration?
3. We may disagree as to our feelings about motorcyclists, but we all agree that a motorcycle driver owes other people the same duty not to injure them as any other vehicle driver does, isn't that so?
4. Will each of you assure me that you will use the good "common sense" you exercise in your everyday life and not ignore your own experience in evaluating the evidence?
5. I take it, then, that if you are satisfied the plaintiff was careless while driving his motorcycle, you will have no hesitancy in returning a verdict accordingly?

COMMITMENT TO OWN VERDICT

1. The defendant is entitled to twelve independent jurors, not merely to two or three who are the most talkative and able to sway the others. Each juror's opinion is important. No one person should dominate, regardless of his or her job, education, or age. Do you believe you can assert your own views?
2. You wouldn't agree with another juror just to please that juror, or to reach a quick verdict, or because you would be embarrassed about stating your own views, would you?
3. Are you willing to stay as long as is necessary to reach a verdict?
4. Is there any pressing business or personal situation that might cause you to want to hurry your deliberations in the jury room?

PERSONALITY CONTEST

1. An unfortunate manner of expression "to win a lawsuit," has been used. You understand, Mr. J, do you not, that we don't "win" lawsuits, since that would imply a game of chance?
2. The outcome of this lawsuit will depend upon hard facts that establish where the truth lies. If, for one reason or another, you happen to like one of the parties or attorneys better than another, it wouldn't cause you to enter a verdict in favor of that party even though the evidence indicated otherwise, would it?

OUTNUMBERED LAWYER

1. As you can see, there are two lawyers representing JD and only one lawyer representing Mr. P. This isn't going to start JD off at a disadvantage with you, is it?

2. Then, I take it, sir, you are not going to feel that in the American spirit of fair play the other side has a handicap and needs your help?

3. And I'm also sure you would agree that the trial of a lawsuit is not a game of sport where one side wins and the other side loses, but, rather, is a process whereby the jury makes an effort to arrive at a verdict on the side of truth and justice. Isn't that correct?

4. Will you assure me that your verdict will be on the side of truth and justice alone and will not be influenced by the number of lawyers on one side or the other?

RESCUING A JUROR FROM DISQUALIFICATION

1. Mr. J, there will be evidence that the little girl I represent was severely injured. I am sure you will agree that we all probably have a natural sympathy for her, isn't that true?
2. Am I correct in stating you will also agree that both sides of this lawsuit are entitled to a fair trial?
3. As a juror, you will surely want to discharge your duties so that both sides to this lawsuit receive fair treatment in your hands, isn't that correct?
4. Do you feel you can properly discharge your duty as a juror by treating both the defendant and the plaintiff with the same fairness and impartiality?
5. Do you have any quarrel with the concept that a lawsuit should be tried free of sympathy or prejudice?
6. At present do you have any prejudice against either side to this lawsuit?

7. Do you know of any reason you cannot give both sides to this lawsuit a fair trial?

8. Is there anything you are withholding or hiding from us that would cause you to have undue sympathy or prejudice for either side?

9. I gather then, you would not be influenced by sympathy or prejudice, and that you would decide this case fairly, solely on the basis of the evidence and the law?

PREVIOUSLY EXCUSED JUROR

Where You Have Excused a Juror in a Prior Case and Now Desire to Keep Him

1. Mr. J, are you the same Mr. J I excused in another case?

2. You realize, do you not, that a juror might be acceptable in one type of case and unacceptable in another?

3. You also realize, do you not, that the fact you were excused is not a personal reflection on your character?

4. Were you in any way offended because I excused you?

5. You wouldn't be against my client, JP, because I excused you the other day, would you?

6. It is very important to JP, so I'm asking you for your solemn promise on this point. Can you give me that assurance?

POLICE WITNESSES
Evaluation of Testimony

1. The police officers who will be witnesses in this case have been named. You understand, do you not, that they are human and subject to making the same mistakes as the rest of us?
2. When an officer is on the stand will you promise to judge him by the same standards you apply to any other witness?
3. The fact that police officers are in uniform doesn't mean they are more apt to tell the truth than anyone else, does it?

Personal Relationship

4. Do you have any relatives or friends who are in law enforcement agencies, such as the F.B.I., a police force, a sheriff's department, or a prosecutor's office?
5. What is your relationship with them?
6. How often do you see them?
7. Do you ever discuss their jobs with them?
8. Because of this relationship, would you find it embarrassing if you were on a jury that acquitted JD?

PRETRIAL PUBLICITY
One Approach

1. Have you heard anybody discussing this case?
2. Have you discussed it with anybody?
3. Have you ever discussed this case with anybody who said to you, "Well, I think JD is innocent" or "I think JD is guilty"?

4. And you, yourself, have not expressed an opinion?
5. It's also true that most of the people who have discussed the case with you were on the side of the police rather than on the side of JD, isn't that correct?
6. As you sat in these discussions, did you at any time suggest that JD might be innocent?
7. In these discussions were you on the side of the police, JD's side, or neutral?
8. How did you first hear or read about this case?
9. What have you heard or read about this case? (This can be a dangerous question. Consider the advisability of asking it outside the presence of other jurors.)
10. Was there anything in the newspaper you read or heard on the radio or television that led you to believe JD was guilty or not guilty?
11. In other words, when you read or heard about this case, you got the impression that JD was guilty, did you not?
12. Weren't the stories on this case slanted on the side of the prosecution?
13. What causes you to believe you are now able to overcome the opinion put into your mind through the news media that JD is guilty?
14. You realize, do you not, that news items or television reports can be unfair or innocently distorted, thereby giving the wrong impression?

A Second Approach

15. Had you ever heard of this case before you came here for jury duty?

16. Is there anything in what you have seen or heard since you reported for jury duty that has caused you to have an opinion about this case, one way or the other?

17. I am going to ask you several questions, the purpose of which is to learn about your own qualifications to be a fair and impartial juror. You understood that, do you not?

18. First of all, do you have an opinion on this case?

19. Have you at any time ever expressed an opinion about this case, one way or the other?

20. Within your own mind, have you ever said, "Well, I think JD is guilty" or "I think JD is innocent"? Have you ever gotten that far?

21. Have you formed any opinion from the news media, newspaper, television and/or radio, that would be a burden JD would have to overcome?

PREJUDICE

1. Would you be inclined to hold the fact that JD is not a citizen against him?

2. The fact that JD comes from Mexico doesn't start him out at a disadvantage with you, does it?

3. JD speaks with a rather broad accent. Will you have patience with him as he testifies?

4. If he fails to completely understand some of the questions asked of him, that will not engender any feeling on your part against him, will it?

5. As you sit here now, do you know of any reason why JD cannot receive a fair trial from you?

COPING WITH BIAS TOWARDS DOCTORS IN MEDICAL MALPRACTICE CASES

1. Mr. J, as you can imagine, this lawsuit is extremely important to my client, JP. We must have jurors who can find against a doctor if the facts so warrant. You realize that, don't you?
2. When you said you could vote for either party, depending on the evidence, you gave the "right" answer. But Mr. J, I'm concerned that you may have a protective attitude of some sort towards doctors who are being sued. Do you think you do?
3. Have you read newspaper and magazine articles which discussed a so-called "medical malpractice crisis"?
4. What influence do you think they have had on you?
5. Did they make you feel a little sympathetic towards doctors in general?
6. Mr. J, we very much appreciate your candor. I know it's difficult to say something that may cause you to be excused. Tell us why you think those articles may have had an influence on you. (Consider asking this question outside the presence of the panel.)
7. Do you feel most suits against doctors are without merit?
8. In this case it is expected that the defense will produce as expert witnesses medical doctors with a long list of accomplishments in the medical profession. Would you let the fact of such accomplishments alone cause you to decide the case in favor of the defendant?
9. Do you think you could find against a doctor if the facts and law warranted such a finding?

10. Do you think you could find against a doctor without secretly requiring my client, JP, to prove his case beyond the amount of proof the law requires?

11. Please Mr. J, think seriously about that point. If you believe down deep you would require JP to prove his case beyond a preponderance of evidence we must know it, even though your honesty will probably cause us to excuse you. Can you decide this case on the same basis as you would any other kind of case?

ADDITIONAL/ALTERNATIVE QUESTIONS FOR PLAINTIFFS IN MEDICAL MALPRACTICE CASES

12. Mr. J, have you or any member of your family ever undergone any type of surgery performed by a medical doctor?

13. What type of surgery was involved?

14. In your opinion, did the surgery save your life or that person's life or eliminate a great deal of pain?

15. In your experience with doctors, have you ever used the expression that a doctor has "performed a miracle" in curing a certain person or member of your family?

16. Please tell us, won't you, your attitude toward a person who files a suit against a doctor alleging medical negligence?

17. Do you believe a doctor is always right?

18. Do you believe a doctor always tells the truth?

19. What is your feeling about whether a professional person should be accountable for negligence of his that causes injury?

20. Do you feel a doctor or lawyer who has been negligent should be exempt from civil liability?

21. Do you have any philosophical objection to such a person having to respond in damages when his negligence has caused injury?
22. As you know, our justice system wouldn't amount to much if jurors who are partial kept their feelings secret. With this concept in mind, can you promise both sides that right now you are as completely neutral as a person can be expected to be?
23. You recognize, do you not, that our decision to accept you or excuse you rests largely on your assurance that you could find for JP if the evidence and the law support such a decision?
24. Do you believe you are just as capable of finding for JP as you are of finding in favor of Dr. D, the defendant, depending only on the facts and the law?
25. Although you are to listen to and consider the testimony and opinions of medical experts, you understand, do you not, that you are not bound to accept their opinions but need give them only the weight you deem them entitled to?

TO ENCOURAGE SELF-ASSERTION

1. Mr. J, I observe that you speak rather softly. I wonder, if you are selected, whether you will be able to speak your mind when deliberations begin?
2. If only one juror's opinion was what the law wanted, we wouldn't need eleven more. The opinions of all jurors are important in reaching a decision. So, if you are selected, can you assure us that you will make your views known to your fellow jurors?
3. Mr. J, when the jury commences its deliberations you will not hesitate to participate in the discussions, will

you? You will speak out and state your views, won't you?

4. Do you believe you can hold to your opinions until such time as you are rationally persuaded to the contrary?
5. You wouldn't change your position simply to go along with the foreman or the majority unless you believed it was right to do so, would you?
6. It is not often that one juror tries to dominate the others, but if it should occur in this instance, will you speak your thoughts and hold your ground until persuaded you are wrong?
7. Wouldn't you agree that a verdict is not just unless it results from each juror's voting in accordance with his conscience?
8. (To the panel) Is there anyone who feels that he or she can't speak his or her mind when the time comes?

QUESTIONS FOR PLAINTIFF'S COUNSEL IN WHIPLASH CASES

The plaintiff often begins whiplash cases at a disadvantage. Many jurors assume the plaintiff is exaggerating for purposes of the litigation. This beginning imbalance may benefit from questioning which meets the issue head-on.

1. Mr. J, this case involves a whiplash injury. You've heard the term used, have you not?
2. Unfortunately for the person who has a legitimate injury, the term whiplash or soft tissue injury has come to connote a faked or exaggerated injury in the minds of many people. You have heard it used in this context, haven't you?

3. But would you agree that some people do sustain serious and painful neck injuries, even though there are no broken bones?
4. How do you feel about people who come to court and claim a whiplash injury?
5. Do you believe, as you sit here now, that you could make a determination of whether JP is faking or has truly been injured, based only on the evidence presented during the trial?
6. In other words, if you have some preconceived notions about the legitimacy of whiplash claims, do you feel you can set them aside and let this case stand or fall on its merits alone?
7. I'm sure you agree that if you are not able to set aside any bias you may have regarding a neck injury, it wouldn't be fair for you to serve on a case like this, would it?
8. Do you believe you could listen to the evidence and make a decision based solely on the facts of this case and nothing else?

A whiplash case is dangerous for another reason. Many prospective jurors have experienced injuries of this type themselves and have recovered quickly and completely. Such jurors will compare your client's situation with their own, and your client is likely to be damaged by the comparison. Try to mitigate the problem by questioning jurors thusly:

9. Mr. J, how long did you suffer from your whiplash?
10. What sort of complaints did you have?
11. Do you have a feeling that because you recovered fairly quickly, everyone else does too? Or do you think that differences in people, in the way accidents

happen, and in the forces involved cause different results in different cases?

12. Why do you say that?
13. I would appreciate your carefully thinking about these questions, because if you would compare JP's injury with your own, I hope you would be forthright and tell us, even though you may be excused. Do you feel you can separate this case from your own?
14. Even though you did not receive compensation do you believe you could award the plaintiff a fair sum if the evidence and law support such an award?
15. You mentioned that your case was settled. Does that mean you received compensation for your injury?
16. Do you think the amount you might award JP would be influenced by the amount you received?
17. Why do you feel that it would not?
18. Do you believe you are capable of awarding JP substantially more or substantially less than you received if the evidence warrants it?

THIRD PARTY CASES

1. JP was injured on the job and was awarded workmen's compensation benefits. Under our laws he may also pursue his right to claim damages from third parties who may have caused his injuries. Do you hold it against him because he is pursuing this right?
2. Are you familiar with the fact that under the law a person can be liable for the acts of another? For example, a principal is liable for the acts of an agent and an employer for the acts of an employee. Do you have any quarrel with this?

3. Under certain circumstances, some duties can be delegated to others to perform, but some duties are nondelegable. The person or company undertaking to perform a particular duty cannot divest itself of liability for the performance of that duty by hiring another contractor or person to perform it. If you are instructed that the defendant in this case had that kind of duty, could you find him liable if the duty was performed by someone else in a negligent manner or not performed at all?